studio international

Visual Arts, Design and Architecture

studio international

Visual Arts, Design and Architecture

Rapid currents in cyberspace

This year serves to prove the non-conformist yet globally enriching characteristic of current interchange in the contemporary art world. This in all the experience across the planet defines a remarkable diversity of ends and means. Yearbook 2006 reveals this, although a similar selection could be made from all the other articles by *Studio International* contributors across the world.

As we look back, it was already fully evident that coverage of China – her history, and her contemporary cultural development – gave a vital new dimension. It is good to recall that *The Studio* – our predecessor, founded in 1893 – took on, through the Founder/Editor/Proprietor Charles Holme (1848–1923) an important commercial and cultural role stemming from his engagement as an entrepreneur in the Far East, becoming a special conduit for ideas. In this, *Studio* was well ahead of other competitors striving to make their mark in this field. Today, doors are opening across all South-East Asia. We were able to document the significant and relevant exchange between London's Royal Academy exhibition 'Royal Academicians in China' (page 70) and the reciprocal show 'China; The Three Emperors, 1662–1795' (page 56) fully approved, and with exceptional loan items, by the Chinese People's Republic. We covered the superb exhibition sent from Vienna to China of 'cutting-edge' contemporary Austrian architecture (page 170), which was exhibited in both Beijing and Guangzhou and has been a further important European inspiration in the run-up to the Olympics. We include the feature article covering Chinese art history (page 8) by Dr Thomas Lawton, former editor for Artibus Asiae, former director of the Freer Gallery of Art and founding director of the Arthur M. Sackler Gallery in Washington, D.C. This is an article of rare insight and research, reflecting Dr Lawton's deep knowledge of the subject.

Drawing down various one-off historical initiatives, we include 19th century paintings by J.C Dahl, as exhibited at the Barber Institute, Birmingham, relating to the Romantic tradition in England and Germany (page 76) and a summary of the Gothic world (page 106), plus a searching essay focused on the 19th century plight of displaced people (page 110). We recognise the contemporary predicament of contemporary artists in Lebanon – as presented by the Museum of Modern Art, Oxford (page 132) – and the real struggle that persists to make art in the Middle East today (pages 156).

Front cover: John Bellany. *Self Portrait In Tuxedo*, Shanghai, 2005. Oil on canvas, 152 cm x 90 cm. Photo courtesy of the Artist. Back cover: Peter Hujar (1934–1987). *Susan Sontag,* 1975. Gelatin silver print, 14 x 14 in. (37.5 x 37.5 cm). Purchase, Alfred Stieglitz Society Gifts, 2006

In London, the dramatic impact of New British Art, as presented at the Tate Triennial 2006 (page 64), could be interestingly set up against the parallel universe of British fashion in our review of the exhibition 'AngloMania' shown at the Metropolitan Museum of Art, New York (page 176). One key design highlight in England was also memorable: the Pallant House Gallery in Chichester (page 152), designed by the veteran Royal Academician Sir Colin St John Wilson, architect of the British Library (d. 2007). This small gem of a building put a historic English cathedral town firmly on the map with a contemporary masterwork that is an exemplary swansong of its designer.

The late Susan Sontag (d. 2004) is commemorated in this 2006 Yearbook by a tribute (page 138) linking her universal talent, as here applied to photography, a key interest for her. We are thankful to the estate of photographer Peter Hujar (d. 1987) for the sublime image by him, which we have incorporated on the back cover.

Michael Spens
Editor

Contributors

Dr Clive Ashwin **CA**	Michael Patrick Hearn **MPH**	Meng Ching Kwah **MCK**	Giles Sutherland **GS**
Richard Carr **RC**	Hwee Koon **HK**	Thomas Lawton **TL**	Christiana Spens **CS**
Sally Davies **SD**	Avril King **AK**	Cindi di Marzo **CDiM**	Michael Spens **Editor**
Mary Ginsberg **MG**	Barbara Kane **BBK**	Dr Janet McKenzie **JMcK**	James Wilkes **JW**
Kanae Hasegawa **KH**			

Contents

Studio
International
Special Issue
Volume 205,
Number 1028
Incorporating
The Studio
founded
in 1893.

Publisher

The Studio Trust
PO Box 1545
New York,
NY 10021-0043
USA

Editor
Michael Spens

Deputy Editor
Dr Janet McKenzie

Creative Director
Martin Kennedy

Vice-President
Miguel Benavides

In Search of China's Imperial Art Collections

On 10 October 2005, the Palace Museum in Beijing and the National Palace Museum in Taiwan both celebrated the eightieth anniversary of the founding of the Palace Museum in Beijing on 10 October 1925. That date, Double Ten 雙十 (i.e. the tenth day of the tenth month), is doubly auspicious in China since the uprising in Wuchang 武昌, Hubei province, on 10 October 1911, also marked the beginning of the revolution that successfully overthrew the Qing dynasty. During the past eighty years there have always been political overtones surrounding control of the Palace Museum since, throughout China's history, possession of the imperial art collections has been regarded as a symbol of political legitimacy. At the dedication ceremony in 1925 Chinese officials stressed the close relationship between the establishment of the Palace Museum and the founding of the Republic.[1] When viewed in the perspective of Chinese history, the Palace Museum collections might be compared to the mythical phoenix in that they, too, have experienced an unpredictable series of rebirths.

To understand public attitude toward the Qing imperial art collections after the establishment of the new republic, it is important to remember how unsettled China was in the years before and after the 1911 revolution. As the new republican government struggled to gain political control of the country from contending warlords whose troops dominated various regions of the country, cultural relics were stolen and sold, and some imperial tombs – including those of the Emperor Qianlong 乾隆 (1711–1799; reigned 1736–1796) and the Dowager Empress Cixi huangtaihou 慈禧皇太后 (1835–1908) – were looted.[2] Factions loyal to Puyi 溥儀, the last Manchu emperor (1906–1967; reigned 1908–1912), tried to thwart efforts to establish a new national museum; with some people going so far as to suggest the imperial collections should be dispersed and sold.

An incident that occurred on 23 April 1926, shortly after the Palace Museum had opened to the public, provides a clear indication of the attitude of some military personnel. Troops from the Hebei and Shandong armies surrounded the palace compound in an attempt to commandeer the area. Two officers accompanied by bodyguards drove their military vehicles up to the Shenwumen 神武門 ('Gate of Divine Prowess'), the north gate of the Forbidden City, stated that they wanted to inspect the palace grounds and ordered that the person in charge should be summoned immediately. The officers and their bodyguards then proceeded to inspect the area, pointing out which buildings could be used for specific military functions and estimating how many troops could be quartered in the various buildings. The person in charge at the Palace Museum immediately reported the incursion to government authorities, emphasizing the historical and cultural significance of the former Forbidden City and stressing that the compound should not, under any circumstances, be taken over by the military. The heads of the two armies professed to

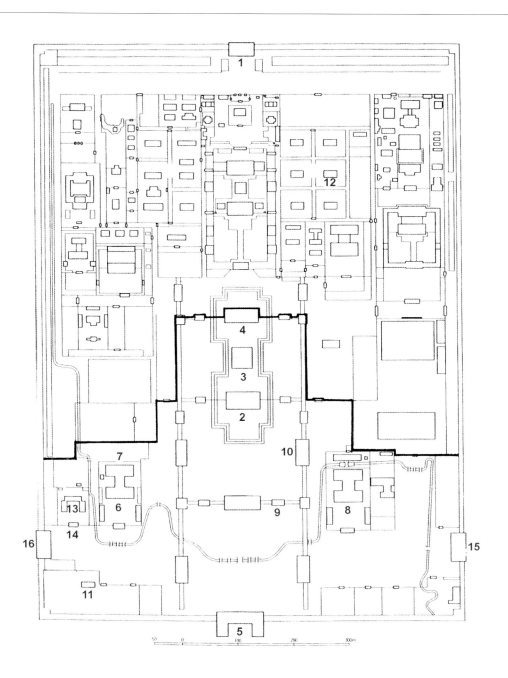

1. Shenwumen 神武門 ('Gate of Divine Prowess')
2. Taihedian 太和殿 ('Hall of Supreme Harmony')
3. Zhonghedian 中和殿 ('Hall of Central Harmony')
4. Baohedian 保和殿 ('Hall of Preserving Harmony')
5. Wumen 午門 ('Meridian Gate')
6. Wuyingdian 武英殿 ('Hall of Military Brilliance')
7. Jingsidian 敬思殿 ('Hall of Respectful Thought')
8. Wenhuadian 文華殿 ('Hall of Literary Splendor')

9. Zhaodemen 昭德門 ('Gate of Clear Virtue')
10. Tirenge 體仁閣 ('Pavilion of Tangible Benevolence')
11. Nanxundian 南薰殿 ('Palace of Southern Fragrance')
12. Yanxigong 延喜宮 ('Palace of Prolonged Happiness')
13. Baoyunlou 寶蘊樓 ('Treasure Storage Building')
14. Xian'anmen 咸安門 ('Gate of Pervading Tranquility')
15. Donghuamen 東華門 ('Gate of Eastern Glory')
16. Xihuamen 西華門 ('Gate of Western Glory')

☐ 1

Figure 1. Plan of the Forbidden City indicating the structures relating to the Bureau of
Exhibition of Antiquities and the Palace Museum. Courtesy Palace Museum, Beijing.

圖全所列陳物古平北部政内

□ 2

know nothing of the matter, saying the inspection must have been carried out by low-ranking officers.[3]

When the Palace Museum opened in 1925 it encompassed only the northern section of the Forbidden City. The circumstances leading to the division of the imperial compound can be traced to the republican government's decision, following the abdication of Puyi on 12 February 1912, to allow the deposed emperor to remain, temporarily, in the northern section of the Forbidden City–that section, referred to as the *neiting* 内廷 ('inner court'), containing the residential quarters of the Qing emperors, their consorts, concubines, and children, as well as of the innumerable servants. The southern section, or *waichao* 外朝 ('outer court'), where the three great ceremonial halls–the Taihedian 太和殿 ('Hall of Supreme Harmony'), Zhonghedian 中和殿 ('Hall of Central Harmony'), and Baohedian 保和殿 ('Hall of Preserving Harmony') – and many smaller structures are located, was placed under the jurisdiction of the republican government's Ministry of the Interior (Figure 1). Government officials began

speculating on possible public functions for those halls – speculations that climaxed in the establishment of a national museum.

The Forbidden City had been 'opened' to the public once before. Early in 1901, following the Boxer Rebellion, the foreign troops that had relieved the siege of the foreign legations in Beijing, entered the imperial compound as a display of strength. On every Tuesday and Friday following that symbolic incursion, Chinese and foreigners were allowed to enter the Wumen 午門 ('Meridian Gate'), the south gate, and depart from the Shenwumen, after having toured the palace compound. That extraordinary opportunity continued only until September of 1901 when the foreign troops left Beijing.[4]

In 1914, eleven years before the establishment of the Palace Museum, the republican government opened the Guwu chenliesuo 古物陳列所 ('Bureau of Exhibition of Antiquities,' hereafter referred to as 'The Bureau'), under the jurisdiction of the Ministry of the Interior, in the southern section of the Forbidden City (Figure 2).[5] In the opinion of one Chinese scholar The Bureau should be

Figure 2. Plan of the structures in the Bureau of
Exhibition of Antiquities. After Duan Yong 段勇,
'Wuyingdian yu Guwu chenliesuo 武英殿與古物陳列所,'
Zijincheng 紫禁城, no. 128 (January 2005), p. 57.
Courtesy Palace Museum, Beijing.

regarded as the first national public museum in
Chinese history.[6] While much has been written
about the history of the Palace Museum, The
Bureau remains relatively little known today,
even though the circumstances relating to its
founding and the sources of its collection are as
remarkable as those of the Palace Museum's
collection. Inevitably, the histories of those two
exhibition areas located within the Forbidden
City are inexorably intertwined.

When the Palace Museum opened in 1925,
the collections on display were selected from
the holdings of the various halls within the
residential section of the Forbidden City. The
collections of The Bureau, on the other hand,
came from the *xinggong* 行宮 ('imperial
summer palaces') in Jehol 熱河 and Fengtian
奉天 (present day Chengde 承德 and
Shenyang 瀋陽), where the Qing emperors had
spent part of each year hunting, participating
in ritual functions, and, not incidentally,
escaping Beijing's oppressive summer weather.

Early in 1913, Zhu Qiqian 朱啓鈐 (1872–
1962), head of the republican government's
Ministry of the Interior, made a decision that
had major implications for the history of the
Forbidden City (Figure 3). Zhu Qiqian's official
position and his impressive family connections
– he was the nephew of Qu Hongji 瞿鴻禨
(1850–1918), a high official during the late
Qing dynasty, and the adopted son of Xu
Shichang 徐世昌 (1858–1939), an important
figure in the Beiyang government in the early
years of the republic – lent added weight to that
decision. Zhu Qiqian had received reports that
some antiquities from the imperial summer

palace in Jehol were being sold by dealers in
Beijing, Shanghai, Tianjin, and Jehol. Rumours
also suggested that Xiong Xiling 熊希齡 (1870–
1942), the *dutong* 都統 ('lieutenant governor')
of Jehol, might have been involved in the theft
and subsequent sale of the antiquities, but
no charges were ever brought against him
(Figure 4).

In the midst of the investigation, Jin Cheng
金城 (1878–1926), an official in the Ministry of
the Interior, suggested to Zhu Qiqian that it
would be an excellent idea to move the
antiquities from the Jehol and Fengtian
imperial summer palaces to Beijing and to
exhibit them in the southern section of the
Forbidden City that was under the jurisdiction
of the Ministry of the Interior (Figure 5).[7]
To support his suggestion, he pointed out that
the southern section of the Forbidden City
would provide an excellent site for a national
museum and, if the site were not put to some
cultural use, it might prove tempting to some
other government agency. Even more
compelling was Jin Cheng's argument that
bringing the Jehol and Fengtian imperial
collections to Beijing would prevent further
thefts and the possibility of additional
important art treasures being acquired
by foreigners.

Jin Cheng had developed a deep interest in
Chinese art as a young man and he expanded
his knowledge of foreign cultural institutions
while studying at King's College, London.
En route home to China in 1905, he traveled
throughout Europe and the United States,
visiting national museums and galleries.

□ 3

□ 4

□ 5

□ 6

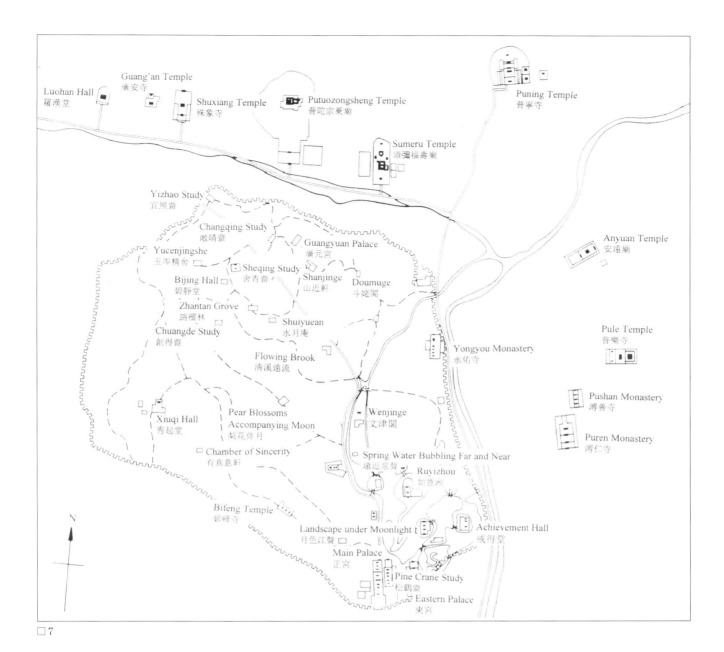

□ 7

Figure 3. Zhu Qiqian 朱啓鈐 (1872–1962). After Duan Yong 段勇, 'Wuyingdian yu Guwu chenliesuo 武英殿與古物陳列所,' *Zijincheng* 紫禁城, no. 128 (January 2005), p. 56. Courtesy Palace Museum, Beijing.

Figure 4. Xiong Xiling 熊希齡 (1870–1942). After *Gugong zhoukan* 故宮周刊, no. 11 (21 December 1929), p. 1. Courtesy Palace Museum, Beijing.

Figure 5. Jin Cheng 金城 (1878–1926). After *Hushe yuekan* 湖社月刊, no. 1 (1927), p. 1. Courtesy Palace Museum, Beijing.

Figure 6. Zhige 治格, first director of the Bureau of Exhibition of Antiquities. After Duan Yong 段勇, 'Wuyingdian yu Guwu chenliesuo 武英殿與古物陳列所,' *Zijincheng* 紫禁城, no. 128 (January 2005), p. 56. Courtesy Palace Museum, Beijing.

Figure 7. Plan of the Jehol imperial summer palace. Courtesy Palace Museum, Beijing.

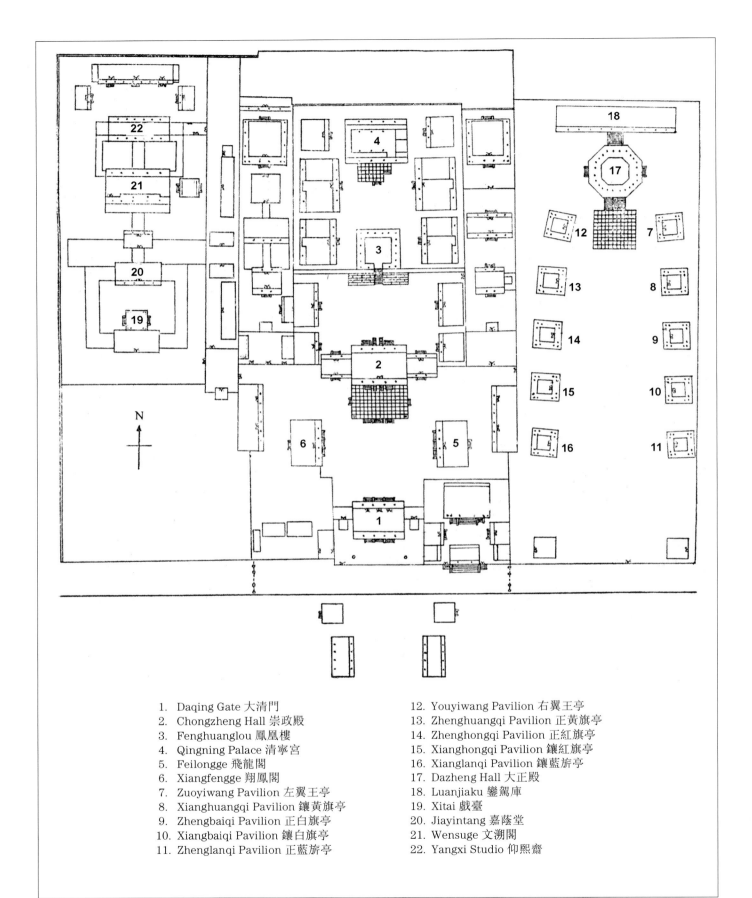

1. Daqing Gate 大清門
2. Chongzheng Hall 崇政殿
3. Fenghuanglou 鳳凰樓
4. Qingning Palace 清寧宮
5. Feilongge 飛龍閣
6. Xiangfengge 翔鳳閣
7. Zuoyiwang Pavilion 左翼王亭
8. Xianghuangqi Pavilion 鑲黃旗亭
9. Zhengbaiqi Pavilion 正白旗亭
10. Xiangbaiqi Pavilion 鑲白旗亭
11. Zhenglanqi Pavilion 正藍旗亭
12. Youyiwang Pavilion 右翼王亭
13. Zhenghuangqi Pavilion 正黃旗亭
14. Zhenghongqi Pavilion 正紅旗亭
15. Xianghongqi Pavilion 鑲紅旗亭
16. Xianglanqi Pavilion 鑲藍旗亭
17. Dazheng Hall 大正殿
18. Luanjiaku 鑾駕庫
19. Xitai 戲臺
20. Jiayintang 嘉蔭堂
21. Wensuge 文溯閣
22. Yangxi Studio 仰熙齋

On his second trip to the United States and Europe as a member of an official government delegation, in 1910, Jin Cheng had another opportunity to observe the organization and functions of foreign museums and galleries. The 1911 revolution had already begun when the delegation returned to China and, during the ensuing governmental reorganization, Jin Cheng joined the staff at Ministry of the Interior.

Zhu Qiqian received Jin Cheng's suggestion with great enthusiasm. In his capacity as head of the Ministry of the Interior, he announced that he was preparing to move the important antiquities from Jehol and Fengtian to Beijing, where they would be exhibited in the newly-established Bureau of Exhibition. He also named Zhige 治格, a member of the Manchu Plain White Banner who had held several important posts, including Vice President of the Office concerned with Manchuria and Tibet, as the first director of the new governmental entity (Figure 6).

Although Jin Cheng deserves credit for proposing the establishment of a national museum, it was Zhu Qiqian who possessed the necessary political influence and connections to ensure the pioneering proposal would become a reality. Using his influence and connections to good advantage, he succeeded in obtaining financial support to initiate the project from the Boxer Indemnity Funds remitted by the United States. As a result of his success in obtaining that support, Zhu Qiqian was referred to as *caishen* 財神 ('God of Wealth').[8] To appreciate the significance of his achievement, it should be noted that Cai Yuanpei 蔡元培 (1868–1940), the Minister of Education, who had proposed establishing a museum of history in 1912, had to wait fourteen years before his proposal could be realized precisely because of a lack of funding.

In the meantime other preparations for the new museum were underway. In October 1913, the Ministry of the Interior dispatched two officials, together with a group of assistants, to the Bishu shanzhuang 避暑山莊 ('Summer Retreat Mountain Villa'), the Jehol imperial summer palace located in Hebei province, north of the Great Wall (Figure 7).[9] The Neiwufu 內務府 ('Imperial Household Office'), representing the interests of the Qing imperial family, also sent two officials and a group of assistants. The entire Jehol complex, built in the years from 1703 to 1790, during the reigns of Emperor Kangxi 康熙 (1654–1722; reigned 1661–1722) and Emperor Qianlong, covers 564 hectares (approximately 1,385 acres) and includes palaces and an extensive series of gardens; the layout of the gardens, with small villas set within bucolic surroundings, was influenced by private gardens the two rulers had seen in Suzhou 蘇州 and Hangzhou 杭州 during their Southern Tours. Outside the ten-kilometer-long meandering wall surrounding the buildings and gardens there are ten Buddhist temples and monasteries. The largest of the temples, the Putuozongsheng 普陀宗乘, was modeled after the Potala in Tibet.

The representatives of The Bureau and of the Imperial Household were responsible for collecting the antiquities dispersed throughout the buildings and supervising their packing for transportation to Beijing. In all there were seven shipments from Jehol, beginning on 18 November 1913 and continuing until 28 October 1914, that required 1,949 crates and included more than 117,700 objects: jades, ceramics, calligraphy and paintings, folding screens, cloisonné, bamboo and lacquer objects, etc. Forty-three live deer were also included with the antiquities. The antiquities and the deer were transported by boat via the Luan River 灤河 to Luanzhou 灤州, and then by rail to Beijing.

The second phase of the project, selection of antiquities from the imperial summer palace in Fengtian, Liaoning province, began in January 1914 (Figure 8).[10] The Ministry of the Interior again sent two representatives accompanied by more than ten cultural specialists, together with ten specialists from the Qibaozhai 奇寶齋, an antique shop in Beijing, who were experienced in wrapping and packing antiquities. The Imperial Household Office again sent its own representatives. Construction of the Fengtian imperial summer palace, which was more modest in scale and more formal in layout than the Jehol complex, had begun in 1636, prior to the Manchu defeat of the Ming dynasty, and continued into the reign of Emperor Qianlong. Beginning on 23 January 1914 and continuing until 24 March 1914, there were six shipments of antiquities from Fengtian, that required 1,201 crates and included more than 114,600 ceramics, ancient bronzes, calligraphy and paintings, jade, etc.

According to one account, the antiquities from the Jehol and Fengtian imperial summer palaces were appraised as having a value of $4,066,047.[11] That same account goes on to cite a formal written agreement, dated 11 September 1916, which states those 'treasures were acknowledged to be part of private property of the imperial family; ...that by mutual arrangement between the imperial family and the republic, all the items except those withdrawn by the former were to be bought by the republican government at the figure named in the valuation; that as financial stringency made it impossible at that time for the republican government to pay the purchase-price, the treasures were to be regarded as on loan from the imperial family to the republic pending a full cash settlement with the finances of the republic permitted'. Apparently the Qing Imperial Household never received any of the estimated $3,511,876 valuation of the antiquities 'on loan' to the republican government.

On 12 January 1914, the Ministry of the Interior announced that The Bureau would include the Wuyingdian 武英殿 ('Hall of Military Brilliance') and the Jingsidian 敬思殿 ('Hall of Respectful Thought'), two adjoining halls in the southwestern portion of the Forbidden City (Figure 9). Once that decision had been made, The Bureau was formally established on 4 February 1914.

Jin Cheng was responsible for overseeing the contracts with companies hired to renovate the Wuyingdian and the Jingsidian, as well as for supervising all aspects of the work. To ensure

Figure 9. The Wuyingdian 武英殿 ('Hall of Military Brilliance'). After Duan Yong 段勇, 'Wuyingdian yu Guwu chenliesuo 武英殿與古物陳列所,' *Zijincheng* 紫禁城, no. 128 (January 2005), p. 24. Courtesy Palace Museum, Beijing.

Figure 10. The Wenhuadian 文華殿 ('Hall of Literary Splendor'). After Duan Yong 段勇, 'Wuyingdian yu Guwu chenliesuo 武英殿與古物陳列所,' *Zijincheng* 紫禁城, no. 128 (January 2005), p. 24. Courtesy Palace Museum Beijing.

□ 9

□ 10

that the materials used in the renovation would be comparable in quality to that in the existing structures, Jin Cheng insisted that most of the properly seasoned wood–*nanmu* 楠木 (Phoebe *nanmu*), *songmu* 松木 (pine) and *shamu* 杉木 (China fir)–should come from older, dilapidated structures located nearby in the southwestern corner of the Forbidden City. From March through November of 1914, the Wuyingdian and the Jingsidian were linked to form an 'I'-shaped unit, and a German firm was hired to adapt the interiors of both buildings to make them suitable for use as exhibition galleries. Other changes were considerably less traditional. The telephone installed in the Wuyingdian and the Jingsidian in May 1914 was the first in the Forbidden City; it was not until 1921 that Puyi had his own telephone. Two months later, following a fire in the southern section of the Forbidden City, running water was installed in the Wuyingdian and the Jingsidian to ensure adequate firefighting facilities.

As the antiquities shipped to Beijing started to arrive, Bureau officials turned their attention to providing adequate storage facilities. Those antiquities that arrived in Beijing during February and March 1914 were stored, temporarily, in the Wenhuadian 文華殿 ('Hall of Literary Splendor'), a large building located in the southeastern section of the complex (Figure 10). When the Wenhuadian was full, and the antiquities continued to arrive in increasingly large numbers, Bureau of Exhibiting Antiquities authorities requested that the Ministry of the Interior also make

□ 11

Figure 11. Drawing of the Baoyunlou 寶蘊樓. After Xu
Yilin 許以林, 'Baoyunlou de jianzhu tese
寶蘊樓的建築特色,' *Zijincheng* 紫禁城, no. 35 (April
1986), p. 32. Courtesy Palace Museum, Beijing.

available to them the halls flanking the
Zhaodemen 昭德門 ('Gate of Clear Virtue')
and the Tirenge 體仁閣 ('Pavilion of
Tangible Benevolence').

On 10 October 1914, The Bureau officially
opened to the public. Although that opening
was a significant event in the development of
national museums in China, public reaction to
The Bureau was not as enthusiastic as it would
be when the Palace Museum opened eleven
years later. The lack of publicity surrounding
the 1914 opening was partly to blame for the
difference in public reaction; in addition, the
greater public interest in 1925 undoubtedly
reflected an understandable curiosity to see
the chambers in which the Qing imperial
family had lived. A further problem was that
the exhibition space initially available to The

Bureau was limited to the Wuyingdian and
Jingsidian. Some critics pointed out that the
first exhibition was installed before the
renovation had been completed; moreover too
many objects were displayed, with too little
explanatory information. Consequently, when
the noted author, Lu Xun 魯迅 (1881–1936),
visited The Bureau, his reaction was that it
resembled an antique shop.[12]

To provide additional exhibition space, the
interior of the Wenhuadian was renovated from
June 1915 to November 1916, thereby providing
public access to the southeastern side of the
complex. At that time the Three Great Halls
were not yet under the jurisdiction of The
Bureau. It was only after Yuan Shikai's 遠世凱
(1859–1916) brief, ill-fated reign as emperor
(12 December 1915–22 March 1916), that the

Three Great Halls were turned over to The Bureau—most of the new space was used to store documents. Many more Chinese and foreign visitors were attracted to those new facilities and, beginning in 1919, the Three Great Halls were occasionally used for special events. However, the decision not to display antiquities in the Three Great Halls meant that section of The Bureau attracted fewer visitors than did the Wuyingdian, Jingsidian and Wenhuadian.

In addition to the antiquities from the Jehol and Fengtian imperial summer palaces, The Bureau was given custody of cultural objects from several other sources, such as imperial portraits formerly housed in the Nanxundian 南薰殿 ('Palace of Southern Fragrance'), a hall located in the southwestern corner of the Forbidden City, and antiquities from the Yonghegong 雍和宮 ('Palace of Harmony and Peace'), situated outside the Forbidden City in the northeastern sector of Beijing.[13] By 1934 the collections of The Bureau numbered more than 280,000 items.

Providing adequate storage facilities for such a large collection had posed a serious problem from the outset. By the time half of the shipments from Jehol and Fengtian had arrived in Beijing, officials from the Ministry of the Interior and the Ministry of Foreign Affairs had approved plans for a new storage facility to the west of the Wuyingdian and Jingsidian, on the site of the former Xian'angong 咸安宮 ('Palace of Pervading Tranquility').

Construction of the new facility, the Baoyunlou 寶蘊樓 ('Treasure Storage Building'), began on 2 June 1914 and was completed in June 1915. Designed and constructed in western style, the building presented a marked contrast to the traditional architecture throughout the Forbidden City (Figure 11).[14] The original Xian'anmen 咸安門 ('Gate of Pervading Tranquility'), which survived the fire that destroyed the Xian'angong in the latter part of the Qing dynasty, provided a secure entrance on the south side of the 'U'-shaped structure. The three-story building and basement were constructed of large bricks that were covered with a layer of cement, which was incised to resemble massive stone blocks. The exterior surface was then painted red; the windows, framed in white, form a contrast with the red walls. Thick ironclad shutters that remained closed throughout the year protected each window. Plaques mounted beneath the projecting roofs of buildings in the Forbidden City, including the Xian'anmen, record the titles of those structures in Chinese and Manchu. In contrast to that tradition, a rectangular stone tablet engraved with the Chinese characters, 寶蘊樓, is set vertically into the courtyard façade of the Baoyunlou. One critic described the Baoyunlou as 'a useful but hideous structure'.[15]

A decade later, when the Palace Museum had to resolve similar storage problems for its most important antiquities, authorities selected the site of the Yanxigong 延喜宮 ('Palace of Prolonged Happiness') on the eastern side of the complex, where the original building was so rundown that it could not be renovated. The reinforced concrete, 'U'-shaped building that replaced the older structure was not unlike the Baoyunlou in its general design and proportions but, as a concession to the traditional style of the surrounding buildings, the roof of this storage facility has a yellow tile roof, with appropriate eave tiles and acroteria.[16]

A series of important, scholarly publications provide a valuable record of some of the objects in The Bureau. The *Neiwubu Guwu chenliesuo shuhua mulu* 內務部古物陳列所書畫目錄 ('Catalogue of Calligraphy and Paintings in the Bureau of Exhibition of Antiquities, Ministry of the Interior'), published in 1925, set a high standard that was maintained throughout the museum's brief history.[17] He Yu 何煜, chief editor of the catalogue, wrote a preface. Gong Xinzhan 龔心湛 (1869–1943), who had been acting premier of China from 13 June to 24 September 1919, contributed the first preface and wrote the calligraphy for the title page (Figure 12).

Among the calligraphy included in *Neiwubu Guwu chenliesuo shuhua mulu* are two quatrains by the Song dynasty Emperor Huizong 徽宗 (1082–1135; reigned 1100–1126) that conclude, 'Dancing butterflies are confused by fragrant pathways; fluttering about, they chase the evening breeze'.[18] The large characters, written on silk in the emperor's distinctive style, characterized by attenuated strokes with contrasting thick and thin elements, and described as *shoujin tizi* 瘦金體子 (or 'slender gold'), are arranged in twenty columns with two characters in each column (Figure 13).[19]

The paintings in the 1925 catalogue include a small hanging scroll, *Jiu sheng huan yu tu*

□ 12

Figure 12. Title page of *Neiwubu Guwu chenliesuo shuhua mulu* 內務部古物陳列所書畫目錄 ('Catalogue of Calligraphy and Paintings in the Bureau of Exhibition of Antiquities, Ministry of Interior'). Calligraphy by Gong Xinzhan 龔心湛 (1869–1943). Courtesy Palace Museum, Beijing.

Figure 13. Emperor Huizong 徽宗 (1082–1135; reigned 1100–1126). *Two Poems* 詩帖卷.
Ink on silk. Detail. National Palace Museum, Taiwan. Courtesy National Palace Museum, Taiwan.

Figure 14. Shen Zhou 沈周 (1427–1509), *Jiu sheng huan yu tu* 鳩聲喚雨圖 ('Turtledove Summoning Rain'). Ink and color on paper. National Palace Museum, Taiwan. After *Baoyun* 寶蘊, vol. 1, no. 7. Courtesy National Palace Museum, Taiwan.

□ 13

□ 14

□ 15

□ 16

鳩聲喚雨圖 ('Turtledove Summoning Rain'), by Shen Zhou 沈周 (1427–1509), rendered in ink and color on paper (Figure 14).[20] The artist defined the turtledove with a simple wash of color and then added a few details in ink; he rendered the bare branch with equally abbreviated ink strokes. In his five-character-line quatrain Shen Zhou asks how the call of a single turtledove is able to summon rain when the chirping of a hundred-bird flock had no effect on cold or heat. The combination of the tersely painted and poetic images lends a Zen-like profundity to the hanging scroll.

The name of the Baoyunlou was used in the titles of two publications that appeared in 1929 and 1930, at the same time The Bureau's rival, the Palace Museum, had undertaken its own publication program. Those two publications also date from the interlude following the overthrow by Jiang Jieshi 蔣介石 (1887–1975) of the Beiyang 北洋 government, which had assumed *de facto* control of Beijing (Figure 15). On 4 June 1928 Jiang Jieshi appointed Yan Xishan 閻錫山 (1883–1960) commander of the Beijing-Tianjin area. In that capacity, Yan Xishan became a member of the Palace Museum Council (Figure 16).

Yan Xishan wrote the calligraphy on the title slip for the first issue of *Baoyun* and contributed an introductory preface, dated May 1930 (Figure 17). Only a few issues of *Baoyun* were published; each one includes twenty black-and-white collotype photographs and brief explanatory comments of a selection of antiquities from The Bureau's holdings. For example, the first issue included the *Songhu*

頌壺, an impressive Late Western Zhou period (9th century B.C.) bronze vessel from the Jehol imperial summer palace (Figure 18). The 151-character inscription cast inside the *Song hu* and its lid records a ceremony that took place in the Zhou dynasty capital during which the Zhou king handed down a charge to an official named Song and conferred a number of royal gifts on him. Song then prostrated himself, and accepted the king's charge and the accompanying gifts.[21] In its size and format, the *Baoyun* resembles *Gugong* 故宮 ('Former Palace'), published monthly by the Palace Museum, beginning in 1929, which also presented a wide range of objects from the collections.

In February 1927, Zhou Zhaoxiang 周肇祥 (1880–1954), then director of The Bureau, had assembled a group of specialists with expertise in ancient bronzes to authenticate the examples in the Bureau of Exhibition of Antiquities. Ma Heng 馬衡 (1881–1955),[22] Rong Geng 容庚 (1894–1983)[23] and John C. Ferguson (1866–1945)[24] were included in the group that met every week for the next two years.

Rong Geng selected ninety-two bronzes from those brought to Beijing from the imperial summer palace in Fengtian for discussion in *Baoyunlou yiqi tulu* 寶蘊樓彝器圖錄 ('Illustrated Record of Ritual Vessels in the Baoyunlou'), a catalogue published in 1929 (Figure 19).[25] Those bronzes had been catalogued earlier in the *Xiqing xujian, yibian* 西清續鑑, 乙編 ('*Western Purity, Supplement II*'), the fourth of the imperial bronze

☐ 17

Figure 15. Jiang Jieshi 蔣介石 (1887–1975). After *Gugong zhoukan* 故宮周刊, no. 4 (2 November 1929), p. 1. Courtesy Palace Museum, Beijing.

Figure 16. Yan Xishan 閻錫山 (1883–1960). After *Gugong zhoukan* 故宮周刊, no. 6 (16 November 1929), p. 1. Courtesy Palace Museum, Beijing.

Figure 17. Title page of first issue of *Baoyun* 寶蘊. Calligraphy by Yan Xishan 閻錫山 (1883–1960). Courtesy Palace Museum, Beijing.

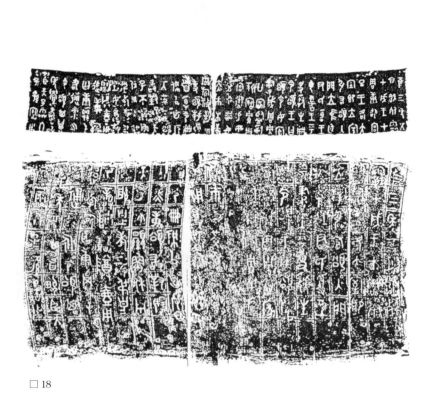

□ 18

compilations prepared during the Qing dynasty. Critics had pointed out the large number of spurious items included in that Qing imperial catalogue, however, and Rong Geng offers refreshingly new analyses.

One of the bronzes selected by Rong Geng is the *Tongshi gui* 同師簋, a Middle Western Zhou dynasty food vessel with a nine-character inscription in which Tongshi expresses the wish that the bronze would be used for ten thousand years (Figure 20).[26] The squat proportions of this covered bronze, the stylized bands of decoration and the modeling of the two handles are typical of ritual bronzes dating from the Middle Western Zhou period (9th century B.C.). Ma Heng, a member of the antiquities section of the Palace Museum who served as director of the museum from 1933 to

1952, wrote the characters for the title slip of Rong Geng's catalogue. Ma Heng's active participation in the authentication and publication program of The Bureau is a clear indication of curatorial interaction between the two museums.

Rong Geng did not include a preface in *Baoyunlou yiqi tulu*, reserving his general comments on the circumstances surrounding that catalogue for the preface of *Wuyingdian yiqi tulu* 武英殿彝器圖錄, ('Illustrated Record of Ritual Vessels in the Wuyingdian') (Figure 21).[27] Deng Erya 鄧爾疋 (1883–1954), Rong Geng's uncle, who was a noted epigrapher and seal carver, wrote the calligraphy for the title slip of *Wuyingdian yiqi tulu*. In that second bronze compilation, which appeared in 1934, Rong Geng selected one

□ 19   □ 20

Figure 17. Title page of first issue of *Baoyun* 寶蘊.
Calligraphy by Yan Xishan 閻錫山 (1883–1960). Courtesy
Palace Museum, Beijing.

Figure 18. *Songhu* 頌壺, Bronze. Late Western Zhou
period (9th century B.C.). After *Baoyun* 寶蘊, vol. 1, no.
15. Courtesy Palace Museum, Beijing.

Figure 19. Title slip of *Baoyunlou yiqi tulu*
寶蘊樓彝器圖錄 ('Illustrated Record of Ritual Vessels in
the Baoyunlou'). Calligraphy by Ma Heng 馬衡 (1881–
1955). Courtesy Palace Museum, Beijing.

Figure 20. *Tongshi gui* 同師簋, Bronze. Middle Western
Zhou dynasty (9th century B.C.). After *Baoyunlou yiqi
tulu* 寶蘊樓彝器圖錄 ('Illustrated Record of Ritual
Vessels in the Baoyunlou'), no. 62. Courtesy Palace
Museum, Beijing.

Figure 21. Title slip of *Wuyingdian yiqi tulu* 武英殿彝器圖錄 ('Illustrated Record of Ritual Vessels in the Wuyingdian'). Calligraphy by Deng Erya 鄧爾疋 (1883-1954). Courtesy National Palace Museum, Taiwan.

Figure 22. Bronze *gui* 簋. Late Shang-early Western Zhou dynasty (11th century B.C.). National Palace Museum, Taiwan. After *Wuyingdian yiqi tulu* 武英殿彝器圖錄 ('Illustrated Record of Ritual Vessels in the Wuyingdian'), no. 54. Courtesy National Palace Museum, Taiwan.

Figure 23. View of Xihuamen 西華門 ('Gate of Western Glory'), with horizontal plaque of Guwu chenliesuo 古物陳列所 ('Bureau of Exhibition of Antiquities'). After Liang Ssu-ch'eng, *A Pictorial History of Chinese Architecture* (Boston: MIT Press, 1984), p. 110, Figure 54. Courtesy Palace Museum, Beijing.

hundred bronzes from the 851 examples brought to Beijing from the imperial summer palace in Jehol, none of which had been previously catalogued. Included among those bronzes is a late Shang-early Western Zhou dynasty ritual food container, type *gui* 簋 (Figure 22), dating from the late Shang-early Western Zhou period (11th century B.C.).[28] Horizontal bands of stylized dragons decorate the bowl-shaped body below the everted rim and on the high ring-foot. Much more conspicuous is the nipple pattern that emerges from a diagonal grid.

Once the Palace Museum was established, important government, military, and financial figures such as Jiang Jieshi, Zhang Xueliang 張學良 (1898-2001), Song Ziwen 宋子文 (1891-1971) and Cai Yuanpei served as members of its advisory committee. As the Palace Museum benefited from the support of its influential council members, the status of The Bureau, which had depended on the support of the Beiyang government, began to decline. During a brief period in 1930, when several warlords joined forces to oppose Jiang Jieshi, The Bureau was free of control by the Nanking government. It was during that period that The Bureau, in an overt expression of its autonomy, added large horizontal plaques over the Donghuamen 東華門 ('Gate of Eastern Glory') and the Xihuamen 西華門 ('Gate of Western Glory') (Figure 23).

After Jiang Jieshi succeeded in overcoming his military opponents, the Nanjing government again assumed its supervisory role. In a number of significant decisions, Jiang Jieshi appointed a new advisory committee for the Palace Museum and gave the Palace Museum authority over a portion of the Forbidden City that formerly had been part of The Bureau. In addition, some of the cultural relics from the Jehol and Fengtian imperial summer palaces were transferred to the new museum Jiang Jieshi was planning for Nanjing. It is significant that in making those announcements, Jiang Jieshi referred to The Bureau as the Guwu baocunsuo 古物保存所 ('Bureau for Preservation of Antiquities'), thereby stressing its function as a storage facility. That subtle distinction was to have still further implications.

After 18 September 1931, when Japanese forces invaded Manchuria and threatened northern China, the Nanjing government made plans to move the imperial collections to Shanghai and then to Nanjing. When Beijing residents protested, saying the government was placing the antiquities ahead of the people, the five shipments were carried out secretly, at night. The first shipment consisted of Palace Museum holdings, the second included objects from The Bureau and the Yiheyuan 頤和園 ('Summer Palace') in Beijing[29] and the Guozijian 國子監 ('Imperial College').[30] In all, the 5,415 crates from The Bureau, contained 111,549 items: 93,707 ceramics, 1,729 bronzes, 786 jades, 2,817 cloisonné, 493 calligraphy and paintings, etc. The bronzes illustrated in the *Baoyunlou yiqi tulu* and *Wuyingdian yiqi tulu* were among those antiquities.

In Shanghai the antiquities were initially stored in warehouses in the French and British

武榮碑額

梁畫長至

鄭□□

□21

□22

□23

concessions where their safety was entrusted to French and British police, assisted by plainclothesmen from the Chinese police. Concerns regarding the possibility of loss or damage as a result of fires, theft or dampness prompted the government to construct modern storage facilities in Nanjing. The new building, constructed of reinforced concrete, was three stories high and, particularly important, was equipped with temperature and humidity controls.[31]

Nanjing was the capital of the Nationalist government, headed by Jiang Jieshi. Planning for a new museum, the Zhongyang bowuyuan 中央博物院 ('Central Museum'), intended as a major institution in the capital that would symbolize the government's support of history, science and culture, with collections including the natural sciences, humanities and technology, began in 1933.[32] Inherent in Jiang Jieshi's decision to establish the Central Museum was the realization that it would add legitimacy to his regime.

The government assembled the antiquities to be housed in the Central Museum from several sources, including purchases from private collectors and transfers of objects formerly in the collections of the Beiping Lishi bowuguan 北平歷史博物館 ('Beiping History Museum'), the Guozijian, and The Bureau. In May 1935, as the Nationalist government considered additional measures to consolidate the various collections of antiquities in Nanjing, it cited the need to reduce expenses and proposed that the Palace Museum should be granted jurisdiction over The Bureau. In response, Bureau administrators appealed that proposal, pointing out many other means by which the government might achieve spending reforms. The government withdrew its proposal and, at the same time, reduced The Bureau's annual budget by twelve percent.

When the Chinese government agreed to participate in the International Exhibition of Chinese Art, held at the Royal Academy in London, from December 1935 through March 1936, the largest portion of the 1,022 antiquities came from the collections of the Palace Museum; The Bureau loaned 57 objects, most of them ancient bronzes.[33] The London exhibition marked the first time there had been such a large loan exhibition of Chinese antiquities outside mainland China and international reaction to Chinese cultural achievements was enthusiastic.

A grant from the British portion of the Boxer Indemnity Fund enabled the Chinese government to construct a properly equipped building to house the collections of the Central Museum. Although construction began in 1936, Japanese bombing of Nanjing forced an end to that work the following year. The staff and collections of the Central Museum, together with those of the Palace Museum and The Bureau, were moved to southwestern China, where they remained during the Sino-Japanese War.[34] When the collections were returned to Nanjing at the end of the war, staff members found that portions of the Central Museum building had been severely damaged, making it necessary to rebuild the structure during 1946 through 1948.

In 1946 the Nationalist government again proposed legislation that would transfer jurisdiction of The Bureau to the Palace Museum. That proposal was finally approved in 1948. Having achieved its goal, the government then made preparations to transfer to the Central Museum all of the objects from The Bureau that had been shipped from Beijing. The twenty-four-year history of The Bureau had ended.

The volatile political situation posed by the Communist insurgency caused the Nationalist government to move the Palace and Central Museum collections once more. During 1948 and 1949 the major portions of those collections were loaded onto ships and taken to Taiwan. Of the nearly three thousand crates shipped to Taiwan, 852 of them contained select objects from The Bureau. The Central Museum objects that were left behind are now in the Nanjing Museum. In an ironic twist of fate, the Central Museum collections taken to Taiwan eventually were joined with those of the National Palace Museum under a joint administration.[35]

Throughout their long, frequently perilous journey throughout China during the decades following 1914–being packed and repacked, passing through one political or military crisis to another–the imperial art collections have maintained their dual role as enduring symbols of political legitimacy for changing governments and as examples, par excellence, of China's unique cultural heritage. Once again those imperial art collections have been dispersed, with the major portions now in Beijing and Taiwan. It is impossible to know what the future has in store for those antiquities; in the meantime, however, they retain their powerful mystique, which continues to evoke both awe and admiration.

Thomas Lawton

Notes
1. For a discussion of the 1925 opening ceremony, together with photographs of some of the speakers, see *Gugong zhoukan* 故宮周刊, no. 1, (10 October 1929), p. 4.
2. For an account of the looting of the mausoleums of Qianlong and the Dowager Empress Cixi huangtaihou by Nationalist troops under the command of Sun Dianying 孫殿英 in 1928, see Gao Boyu 高伯雨, *Qianlong Cixi fenmu bei tao jishi* 乾隆慈禧墳墓被盜紀實. Hong Kong: Dahua chubanshe 大華出版社, 1975; and Yu Shanpu 于善浦, 'Cixi ling beidao shimo 慈禧陵被盜始末,' *Wenwu tiandi* 文物天地, 1981, no. 5, pp. 38–40.
3. Na Zhiliang 那志良, *Gugong sishinian* 故宮四十年, Taiwan: Shangwu yinshuguan 商務印書館, 1966, p. 22.
4. Duan Yong 段勇, 'Guwu chenliesuo de xingshuai ji qi lishi diwei shuping 古物陳列所的興衰及其歷史地位述評,' *Gugong bowuyuan yuankan* 故宮博物院刊, 2004, 5, no. 115, p. 22; Wan Qingli 萬青力, 'Nanfang beijian: Minguo chunian nanfang huajia zhudao de Beijing huatan (shang) 南方北漸：民國初年南方畫家主導的北京畫壇 (上),' *Meishu yanjiu* 美術研究, 2004, vol. 4, pp. 44, 48, 52; and 'Jin Gongbei xiansheng shilue 金拱北先生事略,' *Hushe yuekan* 湖社月刊, 1927, no. 1, pp. 1-3.
5. For a detailed discussion of the Guwu chenliesuo, see, Duan Yong, 2004, op. cit., pp. 14–39.
6. Duan Yong, 2004, op. cit., p. 14.
7. For information on Jin Cheng, see, Yun Xuemei 云雪梅, 'Jin Cheng he Zhongguo huaxue yanjiu hui 金城和中國畫學研究會,' *Meishu guancha* 美術觀察, 1999, vol. 1, pp. 59–62.
8. Duan Yong, 'Wuyingdian yu Guwu chenliesuo 武英殿與古物陳列所,' *Zijincheng* 紫禁城, vol. 128 (January 2005), p. 56.
9. For a comprehensive study of the Jehol complex, see, Tianjin daxue jianzhuxi 天津大學建築系 and Chengdeshi wenwuju 承德市文物局, *Chengde gu jianzhu-Bishu shanzhuang he waibamiao de jianzhu yishu* 承德古建筑-避暑山莊和外八廟的建築藝術. Hong Kong: Sanlian shudian 三聯書店, 1982. For an excellent color photograph of a large hanging scroll (254.8 cm. x 172.5 cm. [approximately 9 x 5 feet]), ink and color on silk, depicting the Jehol imperial summer palace, painted by Leng Mei

冷枚 (active first half 18th century), now in the Palace Museum, Beijing, see, Wan Yi 萬依, Wang Shuqing 王樹卿 and Lu Yanzhen 陸燕貞, *Qingdai gongting shenghuo* 慶代宮廷生活. Hong Kong: Commercial Press, 1985, p. 286, pl. 449.

10. For a discussion of the Fengtian palace, see, Liu Guoyong 劉國鏞, 'Shenyang gugong 瀋陽故宮,' *Wenwu cankao ziliao* 文物參考資料, 1958.3, pp. 59-61.

11. Reginald F. Johnston, *Twilight in the Forbidden City.* London: Victor Gollancz, Ltd., 1934), p. 301.

12. Duan Yong, 2004, op. cit. p. 24.

13. The Yonghegong was built in 1694 as a residence, the Yong Qingwang fu 雍親王府, for Yinzhen 胤禎 (1678-1735; reigned 1723-36) the fourth son of Emperor Kangxi. After the prince ascended the throne in 1723 as Emperor Yongzheng 雍正, his former residence was referred to as the Yonghegong. In 1744 the Emperor Qianlong opened the complex to the public as a Tibetan Yellow-sect Lamasery.

14. For information on the Baoyunlou, see: Li Songling 李松齡, 'Baoyunlou jianzao yuanqi 寶蘊樓建造緣起,' *Zijincheng* 紫禁城, 35, 1986, no. 4, p. 30-31; Xu Yilin 許以林, 'Baoyunlou de jianzhu tese 寶蘊樓的建築特色,' *Zijincheng* 紫禁城, no. 35, 1986, no. 4, p. 32.

15. John Ferguson, 'Bronzes in the Government Museum,' *The China Journal*, vol. 11, no. 1 (July 1929), pp. 22-23.

16. For a description of the Palace Museum storage facility, see Na Zhiliang, *Gugong sishinian* p. 38. For photographs of the interior and exterior of the new building, see *Gugong zhoukan*, no. 209 (7 January 1933), p. 4; no. 210 (11 January 1933), p. 4; no. 211 (14 January 1933), p. 4; and no. 212 (18 January 1933), p. 4.

17. For additional information on the *Neiwubu Guwu chenliesuo shuhua mulu*, see, Hin-cheung Lovell, *An Annotated Bibliography of Chinese Painting Catalogues and Related Texts*, Ann Arbor: Center for Chinese Studies, The University of Michigan, 1973, pp. 94-96.

18. Translation by Charles Mason. For the complete translation, see Wen C. Fong et al., *Possessing the Past* (New York: Metropolitan Museum of Art, 1996), p. 165.

19. *Neiwubu Guwu chenliesuo shuhua mulu, juan 2*, pp. 7a-b.

20. *Neiwubu Guwu chenliesuo shuhua mulu, juan 6*, p. 14a. The painting was discussed earlier by Jin Liang 金梁, in *Shengjing gugong shuhua lu* 盛京故宮書畫錄, preface dated 1913. At that time the painting was stored in the Xiangfengge 翔鳳閣 ('Soaring Phoenix Pavilion'), at the imperial summer palace in Fengtian . See, Yang Jialuo 楊家駱, ed., *Yishu congbian* 藝術叢編. Taipei: Shijie shuju 世界書局, 1962, vol. 21, *ce* 冊 5, p. 17. In his introductory comments to *Shengjing gugong shuhua lu*, Jin Liang states that his compilation includes only the 449 calligraphy and paintings stored in the Xiangfengge; he did not include those examples stored elsewhere in the palace complex. He also comments briefly on other important antiquities housed in the Fengtian imperial summer palace, noting that the bronzes had already been recorded in *Xiqing xujian, yibian* 西清續鑑乙編, and then, in regard to important books, mentions the copy of *Sibu quanshu* 四部全書 housed in the Wensuge 文溯閣, in addition to the volumes kept in the various palace buildings. According to Jin Liang there were 100,000 ceramics in the palace, as well as armor and various kinds of weapons.

21. For a comprehensive analysis of the *Song hu* inscription, see Shirakawa Shizuka 白川靜, *Kinbun tsūshaku* 金文通釋, Kyoto: Hakutsuru Bijutsukan, 1962-, 24:137-164.

22. For information on Ma Heng's career, see, Zhu Jiajin 朱家溍, 'Ma Heng yuanzhang baohu Gugong wenwu de gushi 馬衡院長保護故宮文物的故事,' *Zijincheng* 紫禁城, (February 1986), pp. ; 'Huiyi Ma Heng yuanzhang 回憶馬衡院長,' *Wenwu tiandi* 文物天地, 1987, no. 1, pp. 2-3; Zheng Xinmiao 鄭欣淼, 'Juegong shenwei qide yongxing-jinian Ma Heng xiansheng shishi 50 zhounian 厥功甚偉其德永馨-紀念馬衡先生逝世50周年,' *Gugong bowuyuan yuankan* 故宮博物院院刊, no. 118 (February 2005), pp. 6-23; and several articles in *Zijincheng* 紫禁城, no. 129 (February 2005): Gu Gongren , 'Ma Heng-kuayue liangge shidai de Gugong yuanzhang 馬衡-跨越兩個時代的故宮院長, pp. 6-13; Wang Shuo 王碩, 'Ma Heng juanxian wenwu shangxi 馬衡捐獻文物賞析,' pp. 14-23; Zhang Mingxin 張銘心, 'Juanke yishujia Ma Heng 篆刻藝術家馬衡,' 24-28; Ma Wenzhong 馬文沖, 'Mianhuai xianfu Ma Heng 緬懷先父馬衡,' pp. 29-37; Yan Zhi 閻志, ''Wu Ma' xingkong-hengyu xuejie de Mashi wu kunzhong 「五馬」行空-享譽學界的馬氏五昆仲,' pp. 38-45;

23. For information on Rong Geng, see, Liu Yu 劉雨, 'Daonian zhuming kaogu xuejia he guwenzi xuejia Rong Geng xiansheng 悼念著名考古學家和古文字學家 容庚先生,' *Kaogu* 考古 1983, no. 8, pp. 757-758. For a discussion of one aspect of Rong Geng's research, see, Thomas Lawton, 'Rong Geng and the Qing Imperial bronze collection: Scholarship in early twentieth-century China,' *Apollo*, vol. 145, no. 421 (March 1997), pp. 10-16.

24. For information on John C. Ferguson, see, Thomas Lawton, *The Franklin D. Murphy Lectures XII: A Time of Transition: Two Collectors of Chinese Art*. Lawrence, Kansas, Spencer Art Museum: The University of Kansas, 1991, pp. 65-104.

25. In his text for the *Baoyunlou yiqi tulu*, Rong Geng corrected errors he found in *Xiqing xujian, yibian,*

including questions of terminology, shape, decoration, inscriptions, size and annotation. He includes excellent rubbings of the decoration and inscriptions on each bronze. In spite of the care Rong Geng took in compiling the *Baoyunlou yiqi tulu*, he did not avoid including several spurious vessels, and there are some statements in the annotations that should be corrected. Rong Geng acknowledges those errors in his *Shang Zhou yiqi tongkao* 商周彝器通考 (Beijing: Harvard-Yenching Institute, 1941), vol. 1, p. 201. For an analysis of *Baoyunlou yiqi tulu*, see Shirakawa Shizuka, op. cit., vol. 5, 43:210.

26. The *Tongshi gui* is illustrated and discussed in *Xiqing xujian, yibian, juan* 12:36; and *Baoyunlou yiqi tulu*, no. 62.

27. In his preface to *Wuyingdian yiqi tulu*, Rong Geng mentions that since the bronzes from the Fengtian imperial summer palace had been catalogued during the reign of the Emperor Qianlong, some of them were displayed in the Bureau for Exhibition of Antiquities; since none of the bronzes from the Jehol summer imperial palace had been catalogued previously, they were kept in storage while in Beijing. In his preface to *Wuyingdian yiqi tulu*, Rong Geng stresses the importance of including rubbings of bronze decoration, as well as inscriptions. For an analysis of *Wuyingdian yiqi tulu*, see Shirakawa, op. cit., 43:210–211.

28. The bronze *gui* is illustrated and discussed in *Wuyingdian yiqi tulu*, no. 54.

29. Also known as the Wanshoushan 萬壽山, the Yiheyuan was reconstructed in 1886 through 1891 from an old imperial garden, Qingyiyuan 清漪園, which had been partially destroyed by British forces in 1860.

30. The Guozijian, also known as the Taixue 太學, was an institution of learning for students that included the Biyong 辟雍, where the emperor discussed the Confucian classics with eminent scholars. See Chen Yucheng 陳育丞, 'Guozijian 國子監,' *Wenwu* 文物 1959, no. 9, pp. 37–38.

31. For a description and photographs of the storage building in Nanjing, see Na Zhiliang 1957, pp. 153–154, pl. 6.

32. For detailed information on the Central Museum, see, Tan Danqiong 譚旦冏, *Zhongyang bowuyuan nianwu nian zhi jingguo* 中央博物院廿五年之經過. Taiwan: Zhonghua congshu weiyuanhui 中華叢書委員會, 1960.

33. The Chinese government published a four-volume catalogue of selected objects, *Canjia Lundun Zhongguo yishu guoli zhanlanhui chupin tushuo* 參加倫敦國際藝術國際展覽會出品圖説 ('Illustrated Catalogue of Chinese Government Exhibits for the International Exhibition of Chinese Art in London'). Shanghai: Commercial Press, 1935. Of the 108 bronze ritual vessels illustrated and discussed in volume 1, thirty-six were from the Guwu chenliesuo (referred to as the 'National Museum' in the English-language translation), eight bronzes unearthed at Xinzheng 新鄭, Henan province, were from the Henan Museum's holdings, four bronzes unearthed at Shouxian 壽縣, Anhui province, were from the Anhui Provincial Library's holdings. The 314 ceramics illustrated and discussed in volume 2 were from the Palace Museum. Among the paintings illustrated and discussed in volume 3 are several portraits of early Chinese emperors and their consorts (items 61–62 and 102–103), and a painting by the Yuan dynasty artist, Wang Yuan 王淵 (item 79) from The Bureau. In volume 4, a set of jade seals (item 39), two rhinoceros horn (items 59–60) and a silver sculpture (item 61) were from The Bureau.

34. For detailed discussion of the shipment of the collections to southwestern China, see Na Zhiliang 那志良, *Gugong bowuyuan sanshi nian zhi jingguo* 故宮博物院三十年之經過. Taiwan: Zhonghua congshu, 1957, pp. 172–182; and Na Zhiliang, 1966, op. cit., pp. 86–105. For a brief English discussion of that shipment, see Chu-tsing Li, 'Recent History of the Palace Collection,' *Archives of the Chinese Art Society of America*, vol. 12 (1958), pp. 61–75.

35. Some catalogues published in Taiwan identify the holdings of the Palace Museum and the Central Museum. For example see: *Gugong shuhua lu* 故宮書畫錄. Taipei: Zhonghua congshu 中華叢書, 1956, 4 vols., where the calligraphy and paintings from the two collections are intermixed, with those examples from the Central Museum being identified as 'Zhongbo 中博.' *Gugong tongqi tulu* 故宮銅器圖錄. Taipei: Zhonghua congshu 中華叢書, 1958, 2 vols., where both the Palace Museum and Central Museums are listed as having edited the catalogue; the Central Museum bronzes are presented separately in the second section.

□ 1

Anselm Kiefer: Heaven and Earth

Modern Art Museum of Fort Worth, Texas
25 September 2005–8 January 2006

Musée d'art contemporain de Montréal
11 February–30 April 2006

Hirshhorn Museum and Sculpture Garden, Smithsonian Institution, Washington, DC
22 June–10 September 2006

San Francisco Museum of Modern Art
21 October 2006–14 January 2007

'Anselm Kiefer: Heaven and Earth' is a major retrospective that opened in Fort Worth, Texas. It will travel to Montreal, Washington, DC and San Francisco. Kiefer's paintings, sculptures, books and works on paper have been brought together using the theme of transcendence: 'Heaven and Earth' aptly addresses Kiefer's intention to define the spiritual in art since the mid-20th century. A formidable body of work that resonates in spiritual and material terms, Kiefer's achievements are of great significance.

Based on Germany's physical and cultural landscape since the war, Kiefer addresses guilt, shame and destruction by creating images laden with subtle and personal symbols of rebirth and redemption. Few artists have grasped the constant threat to modern civilisation and succeeded in orienting themselves through a remarkable plethora of visual and theoretical phenomena as Anselm Kiefer. Contemporary art has, in many instances, confused the relationship between art and transcendence, so it is deeply satisfying to accompany Kiefer on his epic journey. Kiefer inscribes a number of his paintings and installations with 'Am Anfang' ('In the Beginning') to stress the need to return to an ancient past, before religious dogma distorted enlightenment. Michael Auping observes, 'Kiefer's road to heaven, informed by an awareness of history, is paved with a scepticism that is turned as much against scientific certitude as it is against theological authority. He does not assume the existence of a paradise, only the ancient need to imagine one'.[1]

'Anselm Kiefer: Heaven and Earth' is accompanied by a Prestel publication of the same title. The book of more than 50 reproductions includes Kiefer's first work, 'The Heavens', as well as many other less known early and recent works that have not been published before. An evocative series of black and white photographs documenting his recent installations in Barjac in France where he works, complete the survey. Kiefer is himself highly articulate and the interview, 'Heaven is an Idea' with Michael Auping, is as an astute a comment on issues of spirituality in art as one might find anywhere. Kiefer is complex and candid, obscure and clear in one. 'Heaven and Earth' presents a most inspiring body of work, international and far-reaching in its scope, a synthesis of abstract pathos and memory.

It has been almost 20 years since Kiefer's work was introduced in America, in a large survey exhibition in 1986–87. Conceived and organised four years ago by Michael Auping, the Chief Curator at the Modern Art Museum of Fort Worth, the exhibition is excellent and the book readable and scholarly. German art since the 1950s has been complex and wide ranging. Michael Werner, the German art dealer, who has organised international exhibitions of recent German art has stated, 'German art of this generation has too many layers and deep, painful splinters to be nursed into order by our generation. This will take a long time, but it must be important because these artists make us fight among ourselves'.[2]

A strong dialogue between American and German art was established after the Second World War. In the late 1950s, American art was

□ 2. Anselm Kiefer. *Resurrexit,* 1973. Oil, acrylic, and charcoal on burlap, 114 3/16 x 70 7/8 in (290 x 180 cm)

marketed as a formidable cultural force. The Museum of Modern Art's major show, 'The New American Painting', championed Abstract Expressionism from the New York School in Europe. It exerted considerable influence in Europe for the next three decades. In the 1980s, the Germans reciprocated the cultural exchange by an exhibition of less cohesive artists that belonged to different generations and ideological standpoints: Joseph Beuys, Georg Baselitz, Anselm Kiefer, Sigmar Polke and Gerhard Richter. A true or complete understanding of the work of such a complex and challenging group of artists eludes the most sophisticated audience to a degree, yet their names evoke solemnity, symbolic complexity and intellectual range. They have become synonymous with the vitality and controversy of art in the late 20th century.

Anselm Kiefer's manifold range of influences is original and illuminating. His recent paintings combine a sensual and passionate affinity with the matiere of paint - its mysterious and symbolic ability to evoke emotional states - to allude to history and layers of meaning, with an intellectual approach that is most impressive. 'For more than three decades Kiefer has explored the dauntingly large question of why concepts such as transcendence and the idea of a superior being exist throughout history.'[3] It has to be said, that given the extreme fragility, complex constructions, and paintings inches deep with paint and objects incorporated, this is an extremely courageous travelling exhibition project.

For German artists since the Second World War, the legacy of Hitler's atrocities cast the darkest of shadows. Both culturally and physically, Germany was in a state of abject despair. Artistic manifestations have been many and varied; Anselm Kiefer's poignant work over the past 30 years signifies the challenge for his generation. 'There is always hope, but that must be combined with irony and, more important, scepticism'.[4] A vision of heaven in today's world, Kiefer believes, can only be achieved if the full weight of history is acknowledged. 'I am not trying to illustrate religion', Kiefer has stated, 'I'm a storyteller with a broken history'.[5]

Kiefer was born in Germany only months before the end of the war in 1945. He studied law before becoming an artist. As a devout Catholic he was interested in the problematic relationship between church and state. Concerned with religious and philosophical issues from his student days, Kiefer brought to art an intellectual rigour that underpins all of his work. When he had studied art at the university in Freiburg, Kiefer had a number of meetings with Joseph Beuys, whose influence gave Kiefer the freedom from artistic convention. Furthermore, Beuys was the first German artist to address the Holocaust in a significant body of work. Beuys stated, 'Everyone went to church, and everyone went to the Hitler Youth'.[6] Central to Kiefer's work has been the use of primal forces and the elements. Fire, with its symbolic associations of destruction, cremation and war, is a pivotal entity in Kiefer's work. Light is used to symbolise God's grace and personal enlightenment. Visions of heaven and hell and hope and destruction are employed by Kiefer in a long and inspiring process to define spirituality, always mindful

☐ 2

3

☐ 4

however, of the state's capacity to use religion as a propaganda tool. Kiefer's landscape paintings are profoundly solemn, eluding to past cataclysm and the inevitability that history will repeat itself.

Kiefer appreciated Beuys' broad-ranging viewpoint, in which history, mythology, religion, and art formed a matrix. Beuys proposed art as a utopian synthesis of various inter-questioning disciplines that was capable of creating an enlightened worldview. While Kiefer was inspired by Beuys' openness and his grasp of a wide range of esoteric knowledge, including alchemy, his viewpoint was less utopian. Beuys became a public figure, while Kiefer would remain far more private and hermetic, with a darker, more sceptical vision. If Beuys was the shaman, Kiefer would be the Gnostic, the questioner of all received knowledge.[7]

Kiefer defined art's role and the role of the artist in a traumatised, post-war world. He incorporates a traditional palette as a symbol to imply the aspiration of art to seek a higher plane, of vision. In the early 1980s, an image of a palette hovers precariously between the physical landscape and the starry heavens. In certain paintings, the palette lies on the messy floor among the detritus of life; in others, it hovers over the physical desolation of Hitler's war. 'In his desperate attempt to communicate beyond the halls of philosophy, church, and state, an artist invariably finds himself in a kind of purgatory.'[8] Referring to his painting, 'The Starred Heaven', Kiefer comments:

I was using myself as the hero of an imagined myth or revolution. It is humorous, pathetic, but it is an important part of researching about who we are in this universe. We are capable of thinking very high and very low. Placing ourselves between heaven and earth is more difficult.[9]

Kiefer uses the natural world as a beginning for his work: trees, forests, life cycles, and the mythology of serpents and angels as a means to create a dialogue between heaven and earth. For Kiefer, the universe contains spirit and matter that are in a continual process of creation and destruction. Fire and melting metals, the combining of metals; transformation and creation are fused. Alchemy is as central for Kiefer, and his work and creativity, as it was for Beuys.

In alchemy, base metals are transformed into gold. The base metal, lead, is used extensively by Kiefer to suggest creativity and spiritual transcendence, much of which has come from the roof of Cologne Cathedral, the tallest Gothic structure in Germany: 'I feel close to lead because it is like us. It is in flux. It's changeable and has the potential to achieve a higher state of gold. You can see this when it is heated. It sweats white and gold. But it is only a potential.

□ 5. Anselm Kiefer. *Quaternity,* 1973. Oil and charcoal on burlap, 117 1/2 x 170 1/4 in (298.4 x 432.4 cm)

The secrets are lost, as the secrets of our ability to achieve higher states seem lost or obscured'. He continues, 'For me, lead is a very important material. It is, of course, a symbolic material, but also the colour is very important. You cannot say that it is light or dark. It is a colour or non-colour that I identify with. I don't believe in absolutes. The truth is always grey'.[10]

Books and book-making form an important aspect of Kiefer's oeuvre: 'For Kiefer, the book has immense symbolic power as a container and transmitter. From the Bible to ancient illustrated manuscripts and books of law, it projects the history of world knowledge. The codifying of laws and languages, the formulation and circulation of theories of creation, the rise of religious and nation-state, and the scientific have played out in books'.[11]

Using impractical materials such as lead, making the pages too heavy to turn, and created on a large scale, Kiefer's books are created primarily for their sculptural and symbolic value. He points out that they are not intended to be read, but to allude to a creative dialogue to symbolise transcendence.

Architectural ruins are used to symbolise human vanity and the ephemeral nature of much of human creation, and the inevitability of destruction. Painted images and installations are created over long periods of time layering sand, ash, earth and emulsion, and then left to age and weather. Keifer states: 'Each of these buildings has a history created by its own fiction and need to demonstrate its philosophy of existence. That fiction is part of the debris of history. My images connect with that debris. They attempt to connect with the beginning or the end, with a deep and lost memory between here and there'.[12]

When Wassily Kandinsky wrote Concerning the Spiritual in Art at the beginning of the 20th century, abstraction seemed the most viable art form. As art in that century developed, there was a tendency for abstract art to degenerate into a mannered formalism, devoid of historical, political or spiritual significance. Kiefer's work employs abstraction with a conceptual awareness that at every point he infuses with an original intellectual commitment. Symbolic materials, found objects, a collection of pieces that represent the minutiae of life but allude to the primal issues of human existence, are all collected, stored and employed like the lost images from one's personal past and from history. The grey minimal canvases, built up from layers of impastoed chunky materials, destined to break away from the painting in time, convey a message direct to the subconscious, enlightening the present physical moment in life, reminding one that however grim the past and future may be, the search, the journey, and believing in both is fundamental to being human, and that art has a pivotal role to play. **JMcK**

References
1. Auping M (ed). *Anselm Kiefer: Heaven and Earth.* London: Prestel, 2005: 50.
2. *Ibid:* 23.
3. *Ibid:* 24.
4. *Ibid:* 27.
5. *Ibid:* 48.
6. *Ibid:* 31.
7. *Ibid:* 31.
8. *Ibid:* 34.
9. *Ibid:* 34.
10. *Ibid:* 37–39.
11. *Ibid:* 40.
12. *Ibid:* 41

□ 5

Hiroshi Sugimoto: End of Time

Mori Art Museum, Tokyo

17 September 2005–9 January 2006

Hirshhorn Museum and Sculpture Garden, Smithsonian Institution, Washington, DC

16 February–14 May 2006

☐ 1. Hiroshi Sugimoto. *Mathematical Form, Surface,*
0004. Onduloid: a surface of revolution with constant non
zero mean curvature 2004. Gelatin-silver print, 149.2 x
119.4 cm. © Hiroshi Sugimoto

□ 1

The first comprehensive retrospective of Japanese artist Hiroshi Sugimoto's work to take place in his homeland, Japan, opened in September 2005 at the Mori Art Museum in Tokyo. Running until 9 January 2006, the Mori exhibit focuses on Sugimoto's photographic work from the 1970s to the present and includes the world premiere of his 'Colours of Shadow'; a new series of colour photographs highlighting the changing light in Sugimoto's studio. Visitors to the show will become acquainted with one of Japan's most versatile multimedia artists of the past 30 years, whose work includes 'Dioramas', 'Seascapes', 'Theatres' and his recent fusion of photography with architecture and traditional Noh theatre.

Initially, the Sugimoto retrospective was conceived by Kerry Brougher, Chief Curator at the Hirshhorn Museum and Sculpture Garden in Washington, DC. Brougher's plans finally came together in 2001, when David Elliott was appointed Director of the Mori Art Museum. Together, Brougher and Elliott spent nearly five years organising the exhibit. Sugimoto designed the exhibition, which includes a Noh stage on which visitors can view a Noh play. A sound installation created by the artist and internationally known sound artist, Ryoji Ikeda, is also on site.

There are more than 100 photographic works on view that reflect the artist's use of the camera to capture the interfacing of memory and time. The development of the digital camera has allowed photographers to create a complete record of visual experience. No longer limited to representative impressions, photographers can capture the fleeting moments that form the fabric of experience. Nevertheless, Sugimoto adheres to the traditional photographic method of making a silver gelatine print using technology invented by Louis Jacque Mande Daguerre in the mid-19th century. In his catalogue essay, Sugimoto says that photography is not just a means of recording what lies in front of us; it can also be used as a tool for self-interrogation, a process in which a person can question what is real and what is illusion.

Born in 1948 in Tokyo, at the close of World War II, to a prosperous merchant's family, Sugimoto was given much freedom and encouragement by his parents. His father gave him his first camera at the age of 14. Curious and intelligent, Sugimoto was drawn to science and technology. At the end of the 1960s, when student unrest was widespread in Japan, Sugimoto chose to study abroad at the Art Center College of Design in Los Angeles, and enrolled in the photography department. Now, after working in photography for more than a quarter of a century, Sugimoto's work is purchased by important collectors. Designer Louis Vuitton, Foundation Cartier and Deutsche Bank are among his clients. According to Sugimoto, the timing of this retrospective is apt. At a press conference, the artist said, 'In the past, I was still not ready for it, but now that I am reaching the age of 60, I thought I might have a chronology of my works that I can show to the public'.

Sugimoto's knowledge of architecture can be detected in his design of the 2,000 square metre

☐ 2

☐ 3

□ 4

□ 4. Hiroshi Sugimoto. *Caribbean Sea,* Jamaica, 1980.
Gelatin-silver print, 119.2 x 149.2 cm. © Hiroshi Sugimoto

□ 5. Hiroshi Sugimoto. *Al Ringling Baraboo,* 1995. Gelatin-
silver print, 42.3 x 54.2 cm. © Hiroshi Sugimoto

□ 5

exhibition space, which is divided into four L-shaped galleries. Entering the first gallery, a 6 metre-high rectangle, visitors encounter two areas with vast white screens standing solemnly like columns in a temple. The screens form an enclosed walkway. At this point, no photographs are apparent. When visitors have walked through the screens and look back, they see photographs of Sugimoto's recent series, 'Conceptual Forms', hanging on the back of the screens. The placement of the photographs suggests that, normally encountered by viewers as they move towards the images, they present a view into the past, or a 'backward' view.

The 'Conceptual Forms' series consists of black-and-white photographs of plaster models that demonstrate mathematical formulae brought to Japan from the West during the early 20th-century Meiji period. These models are preserved at the University of Tokyo. During 2004, Sugimoto began photographing the plaster sculptural renderings. He has photographed the plaster models against a black background as if to monumentalise the forms. In his photographs, the artist offers viewers a visual image for mathematical equations and theoretical knowledge that may have been imparted in school and not tangible reality.

A quest for the veracity of experience and the nature of reality can be detected in each piece on view. In his essay, Sugimoto mentions that, 'Even when I was a school kid, my favourite bedtime stories were not fairy tales, but factual accounts. Nights when I could not go to sleep, I would beg my grandmother for the real-life stuff'. The artist's investigation of what is real

□ 6

□ 7

and what is not is cleverly rendered in his 'Diorama' series, which the artist began at the start of his career. Sugimoto left Los Angeles for New York City in 1974. A pivotal moment in his career took place there when he visited the American Museum of Natural History. Sugimoto explains that when he stood in front of the dioramas, where stuffed animals and such early humans as Homo sapiens appeared in front of painted backdrops, he was struck by their fabricated appearance. However, when he closed one eye and looked at the dioramas from the one-eye point of view of a camera, what seemed to have been fake appeared to be real. Sugimoto has continued to photograph the dioramas in the museum - his most recent diorama is dated 1999.

In effect, Sugimoto is like an alchemist who takes something that does not exist and convinces his audience that it is real. Since each person's perception of the world relies on his or her experience and memories, the notion of what is 'real' is personal. Visitors to the same gallery, looking at the same painting, will view and appreciate the painting in different ways, due to a number of factors that change with each viewer: age, race, culture, religion and education. Similarly, people living in the 21st century have very different perceptions from people who lived 2,000 years ago. For example, with his iconic 'Seascape' series, Sugimoto invites viewers to consider the sea and the sky in the way that ancient peoples might have seen and experienced them. To create 'Seascape', Sugimoto travelled throughout the world for 30 years and chose to photograph places with a similar tranquil quality. He framed each view of the sea and the sky in the same composition, divided precisely in two by the horizon.

While Sugimoto is, indeed, an innovative and remarkably versatile artist, there is a refreshingly down-to-earth inquisitiveness apparent in his work. Like many boys, Sugimoto was fascinated by the speed of railway trains. He collected miniature toy trains and crafted plastic models. To more precisely replicate a train, he took photographs to record a fleeting train. The young Sugimoto was also thrilled to see moving images at the cinema. His idol at that time was Audrey Hepburn. From his fascination with the actress, he decided to photograph an entire movie featuring her, by fixing the shutter of the lens with a wide-open aperture. Because Sugimoto literally took a picture of 'the length' of the movie with an 8" x 10" wide format camera without closing the shutter, there is a span of time condensed in Sugimoto's photographs for his 'Theater' series.

Certainly, the conceptual framework behind Sugimoto's method is intriguing, but the importance of his work transcends the concept. The artist has given himself, and his audience, a glimpse of the nature of reality, the underpinning of all true human experience, and a taste of where self-interrogation can lead. After making the journey through the exhibition, viewers may well start to view the world as Sugimoto does through his camera lens. As the artist says, 'The human eye, devoid of the shutter, is essentially a camera with long exposure'. **KH**

□ 1

Tadeusz Kantor

It is a measure of the seriousness with which many Poles regard culture that the national quality daily newspaper, *Gazeta Wyborcza*, recently devoted a pull-out supplement marking the 15th anniversary of the death (on 8 December 2005) of the director and artist, Tadeusz Kantor.

Kantor, who was born in Wielopole in 1915, came to represent the Polish post-war avant-garde and his theatrical productions - in particular 'The Waterhen', 'Lovelies and Dowdies' and 'Let the Artist Die' - have come to be seen as artistic works without parallel. Even now, their aesthetic radicalism is beyond compare, and their analysis and description have engendered a new critical language.

Kantor lived and worked for most of his life in the city of Kraków – the ancient capital of Poland and seat of the Jagiellonian dynasty. Kraków was rare among Polish cities in that it survived the Second World War intact, because Nazi policy was to annex the city with minimum damage to its architectural fabric.

Therefore, it was fitting and necessary that this city should have hosted a series of events marking Kantor's untimely death. An international symposium was complemented by an exhibition in the Krzysztofory Gallery, documenting the artist/director's links with Germany and Switzerland - as well a show of props and photographs in the Cricoteka, Kantor's archive.

I was first exposed to the work of Kantor in 1989 by the inimitable Ricky Demarco, who led one of his many expeditions to the country. A meeting with Kantor was on our itinerary, and it was a bitter disappointment when the meeting did not take place, as it was undoubtedly the highlight of the journey. What has stuck in mind throughout those intervening years was the story of the 15th-century German artist, Wit Stwosz, who had travelled from Nürnberg to Kraków to escape paying a debt, but who was captured and punished by having a nail driven through his cheek. Stwosz designed and made the magnificent triptych altarpiece in St Mary's Basilica in Kraków's main square. Kantor employed the latent and layered symbolism of the Stwosz story in his theatre-work 'Let the Artist Die'. In Stwosz's suffering, Kantor saw the suffering of artists (and his own), and the story was an apt and enduring metaphor.

The organisers of the symposium should have borne this story in mind when programming the event. Like many other similarly well-intentioned events, it was too tightly packed, with little room to breath (both literally and figuratively). A short walk across the square to the Stwosz altarpiece may have restored many, and fortified them against the series of academicised and ponderous offerings that comprised the majority of the event.

In truth, I gave up and left, and with the help of friends, including Ricky Demarco, made up my own Kantor 'programme', in no small part due to the fact that the proceedings were conducted entirely in Polish and German, with no English translation. Where the head had

□ 1. *Sculptural Chair.* Designed by Tadeusz Kantor and installed after his death in the garden of his country house in Hucisko, near Krakow

Richard Long: The Time of Space

Haunch of Venison, London

3 January–10 February 2006

Since 1967, Richard Long has used walking as the basis of his artistic practice. What appears in the gallery may be a sculpture constructed from natural materials, a photograph of a sculpture made *in situ,* or a text, but none of these would be possible without the artist's walks: the experience of time and motion in the landscape finding its mode of expression and memorial.

His most recent exhibition, at the Haunch of Venison gallery in London, is spread over three floors. The first floor displays three photos taken during the course of a 15-day walk in the semi-desert Karoo region of South Africa. 'Flash Flood' proclaims its title over a dark foreground of scrub, while storm clouds sweep dramatically across the ridges - almost a title still from a film. The other two photographs document sculptures Long has created: in 'Karoo Crossing', by scuffing into definition and bordering with stones two meandering and intersecting paths, and in 'Stones and Stars' by setting stones on end on a hillside. Both sculptures seem to have a greater affinity with naturally occurring shapes than with ancient earthworks: the crossing is reminiscent of a microscopic image of a chromosome, while the vertical stones resemble a small colony of cacti growing among other desert plants.

Just before the stairs is the first text piece in the exhibition, 'Walking Music'. This details, in green and orange lettering, six songs, 'In mind each day', as Long walked for six days through Ireland, 'from the Blackwater River to the Burren to the Athenry'. The songs range from the traditional air, 'Roisin Dubh', to Johnny Cash's 'I Still Miss Someone', via the Beatles' cover of 'Rock and Roll Music'. The titles and musicians' details are mysterious, leaving the viewer to guess whether Long tuned in to some psychogeographical resonance that brought the songs spontaneously to mind, or whether he compiled a virtual tape before he set out, and then silently repeated his musical mantra as he walked.

On the first floor, there is another text piece, 'Walking in a Moving World'. Beneath the title are six lines:

BETWEEN CLOUD SHADOWS
INTO A HEADWIND
ACROSS A RIVER
THROUGH SPRING BRACKEN
UNDER A BEECH TREE
OVER A GLACIAL BOULDER

They offer an unexpected, Haiku-like opening: the glacial boulder moves as cloud shadows do, and here is Long, the subject, another movement in a moving world.

□ 1. Richard Long. *Burlington Northern,* 2003. Photography and text, 129.5 x 88 cm/51 x 34.6 in. Courtesy: Haunch of Venison, London. © Richard Long, 2005

☐ 1

FLASH FLOOD

A FIFTEEN DAY WALK IN THE LOCALITY OF GUARRIE BERG IN THE KAROO   SOUTH AFRICA 2004

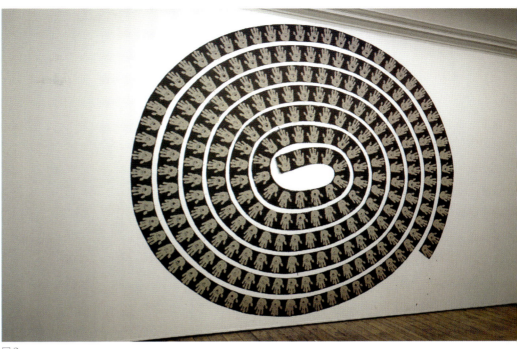

☐ 3

I wasn't so keen on other textual works in the exhibition. 'From Simplicity to Complexity' lists short words progressing down the wall next to the vertical statement 'A STRAIGHT WALK ACROSS DARTMOOR'. It begins with 'ADRENALIN/HOOFPRINTS/LARKSONG', but soon, generalities start drifting in: 'AN IRON TASTE/SENTIMENT/A SNOOZE/SADNESS/HOT FEET/ TUSSOCKS/REGRET'. I would have preferred greater verbal rigour: larksong, an iron taste, tussocks and even hot feet have a certain specificity and power, but not sentiment, sadness and regret. These latter are emotional shorthand, not observation.

Paradoxically, I enjoyed 'Ocean to River' almost in spite of the text. Under the large printed banner of 'OCEAN TO RIVER/WATER TO WATER' was the following small print: 'Atlantic water from the Pointe Espagnole carried across France on a walk of 473 miles in 16 days and poured into the Rhône river at Pougny-Gare at the end of the walk, spring 2005'. Sometimes, Long's actions speak louder than his words.

The top floor of the gallery contains three large sculptures. Standing in front of a piece such as 'Sardinian Cork Arc', looking at the textures and arrangement of the curls of lichen-shaded bark, gives a very immediate pleasure. And yet,

these works, constructed from materials very far removed from their source, are somewhat at odds with the rest of Long's practice, which usually involves a minimal disturbance of the environment. The black and white print of 'The Time of Space' illustrates this: it shows a circle of stones on a gentle screen slope, arranged by Long on a three-day walk on Mount Parnassus in 1999. The caption informs us that he dispersed the circle on a six-day walk in 2002, thus creating 'A CIRCLE OF 1,114 DAYS'.

The sense of pilgrimage and isolation within Long's works and walks lends them power, but this is hard to achieve without selectively ignoring human presences in the landscape. So, it was heartening to find, in the text piece 'All Ireland Walk', amusing fragments like 'IT'S GOING TO BE BAD ALL DAY AND TOMORROW', 'FOLLOWED BY A DOG FOR FIVE MILES', and 'PLEASE LOOK FOR A LOOSE HORSE', giving a more balanced sense of a lived-in land. However, I still feel that there's an unresolved tension between Long's solitary walks through remote areas of the planet, and the display of the resultant art in urban centres. These are places polluted and pollinated, compromised and fertilised by just those factors his walking tries to escape: human contact, exchange and exploitation. **JW**

China: The Three Emperors, 1662–1795

Royal Academy of Arts, London

12 November 2005–17 April 2006

'An exhibition is a display, a performance ... and in "China: The Three Emperors, 1662-1795", we are presented with paintings, dress, porcelains, lacquers and furnishings that the rulers themselves employed in elaborate performances.'[1] So explains Dame Jessica Rawson, mastermind of the dazzling assemblage at the Royal Academy until 17 April 2006. While there have been about 80 exhibitions of Qing Dynasty material from the Palace Museum since 1974,[2] this specifically focuses on the many roles required to be played by the Manchu emperors and the settings in which they played them.

The emperors onstage are Kangxi (r. 1662–1722), Yongzheng (r. 1723–35) and Qianlong (r. 1736–95). Kangxi completed the conquest of the Ming and balanced numerous nationalities and factions, achieving political stability in his long reign. Yongzheng was an autocrat: a suspicious, bureaucratic manager, whose unattractive methods yielded order and prosperity in just 13 years on the throne. For the remainder of the 18th century, Qianlong ruled over Sheng Qing, the 'flourishing' or 'splendid' phase of the Qing Dynasty. The exhibition devotes a room to each of the emperors and his special interests, but the first sections set out the functions and ceremonies of imperial rule.

We first see the emperors in near life-size ancestral portraits, formally dressed in imperial yellow dragon robes. There is also a portrait of the Qianlong's birth mother, the Xiaosheng Empress Dowager, to whom he was greatly attached. These paintings were used in rituals after death, so, as Professor Rawson pointed out in a recent lecture, we are actually beginning at the end.

Splendid imperial garments also hang in the entrance gallery, giving an idea of the grandeur to come. More textiles are on view in the 'Ritual and Religion' sections, and are among the most exciting objects in the show. A pale blue ('moon white') robe is displayed with the matching ceramic vessels used in annual rituals at the altar of the Moon. A magnificent ceremonial costume for an imperial lama comprises a collar, sleeves, skirt and beaded apron of stained ivory beads.

The court paintings dominate the exhibition. To have so many of these grand works in one place is a major occasion by itself. Many are huge. The emperors are shown in a host of guises: military hero, sportsman, religious devotee, imperial lord receiving tribute, festival celebrant, family man, quiet scholar. Qing court

□ 1

□ 2

□ 1. Anonymous court artists. *Portrait of the Kangxi Emperor in Court Dress,* late Kangxi period (1662–1722). Hanging scroll, colour on silk. 278.5 x 143 cm. The Palace Museum, Beijing

□ 2. James Cox (d.c.1791) *Clock in the shape of a crane carrying a pavilion on its back,* 18th century. Gilt bronze and coloured stones. Height 40 cm. The Palace Museum, Beijing

□ 3. *Decorative flattened flask (bianhu) in the shape of an ancient bronze,* Qianlong period, 1736–95. Copper decorated with cloisonnÈ enamel with gilding. 21.9 x 23.3 x 8.5 cm. The Palace Museum, Beijing

□ 3

□ 4

□ 4. *Ceremonial costume for an imperial lama: collar, sleeves, skirt and beaded apron,* 18th century. Embroidered silk and stained ivory, skirt 96 x 80 cm, sleeve length 58 cm. The Palace Museum, Beijing

□ 5. *Teapot and cover,* Yongzheng period 1723–35, Jingdezhen, Jiangxi Province. Porcelain with monochrome celadon glaze. Height 12.2 cm. The Palace Museum, Beijing

□ 6. Anonymous court artists. *From Twelve Beauties at Leisure Painted for Prince Yinzhen, the Future Yongzheng Emperor, late Kangxi period* (between 1709 and 1723). One of a set of twelve screen paintings, ink and colour on silk. 184 x 98 cm. The Palace Museum, Beijing.

paintings documented the emperors' power and legitimised it. In the era before photography, they also recorded as history important court and ceremonial events, and 'scenes of community life', and are essential to our knowledge of this time in China.[3]

Among the painted chronicles is one of the 12 horizontal scrolls entitled The Southern Tour of the Kangxi Emperor, by Wang Hui (1632–1717) and other court painters. They show in exquisite, lively, day-by-day detail the events of Kangxi's grand inspection tour of 1689. The scroll at the Royal Academy is the 11th Nanjing to Jinshan.[4]

Some 70 years later, the Qianlong Emperor commissioned a 12-scroll record of a southern inspection tour. The last scroll illustrating this expedition is also on display at the Royal Academy. By that time, Western influence is clearly visible in the painters' use of linear perspective and foreshortening. Unlike other Chinese scrolls, where the action moves as the scroll unrolls, from right to left, this one shows the emperor moving in the opposite direction as he returns to the Palace.[5]

One of the most important themes here is East-West interaction: diplomacy, trade and learning. The emperors of China, meant to

□ 5

□ 5

possess all knowledge and fulfil all roles, made selective use of Western innovation and artistry. The Jesuit painter, Giuseppe Castiglione (1688–1766, Chinese name Lang Shining), arrived in China in 1715 and served under all three emperors. He married Chinese subjects with Western technique. 'Pine, Hawk and Glossy Ganoderma', in which a white hawk represents the Yongzheng Emperor, is a very fine painting, full of Chinese auspicious and political symbolism, executed in Western style.[6] In another of the many Castigliones on view, Qianlong appears as a youthful military commander. What is surprising about this portrait is that the Emperor is on horseback - this was quite typical in the West, but previously not seen in China.

   Kangxi, among the greatest of all Chinese rulers, was a man of learning and culture. He commissioned grand publishing projects, established the imperial workshops in the Forbidden City and learned science from the Jesuits. The room devoted to Kangxi at the Royal Academy features books, his own calligraphy and a large number of scholars' articles. A porcelain brush pot and wrist rest are decorated as an ink painting of bamboo in the literati style. A stunning set of peach-bloom

□ 7

□ 8

□ 9

☐ 7. Anonymous court artists. From *Album of the Yongzheng Emperor in Costumes,* Yongzheng period (1723–35). One of 14 album leaves, colour on silk. 34.9 x 31 cm. The Palace Museum, Beijing

☐ 8. Giuseppe Castiglione (Chinese name Lang Shining, 1688–1766). *Pine, Hawk and Glossy Ganoderma,* 1724. Hanging scroll, colour on silk. 242.3 x 157.1 cm. The Palace Museum, Beijing

☐ 9. Giuseppe Castiglione (Chinese name Lang Shining, 1688–1766) and others. *The Qianlong Emperor Hunting Hare,* 1755. Hanging scroll, colour on silk. 115.5 x 181.4 cm. The Palace Museum, Beijing

☐ 10. *Vase with butterflies and flowering peach branches, Yongzheng period,* 1723–35. Jingdezhen, Jiangxi Province Porcelain with famille-rose enamels. Height 38 cm. The Palace Museum, Beijing

monochrome porcelains exemplify the technical advances achieved in ceramics of this period.

Yongzheng's reign was very short, and he is the least known to us of the three emperors. He may have been eccentric, but was the real art-lover among them. His reign brought new designs and technical innovations, but 'the results are more immediately associated with Qianlong than Yongzheng, since the son knew how to link his own persona indelibly to this impressive heritage'.[7] A celadon teapot, in a shape unknown before Yongzheng, is perfect in its apparent simplicity (but reveals great technical difficulty).

Two sets of paintings need mention here. Firstly, the highly imaginative, if not eccentric, album of Yongzheng in 13 different costumes: Daoist practitioner, European sportsman and Mi Fu practicing calligraphy, to name a few. The intent of this album is the subject of much unresolved scholarly debate.[8]

The Yongzheng Emperor's 'Twelve Concubines' provides another mystery. Were these Yongzheng's concubines or serving women? These beauties are all dressed in Ming court costume, which was strictly forbidden to Manchu palace women.[9] Whoever the models are, their settings are a fantastic source of information about palace interior decoration and display.

Qianlong's reign has been described as a period of 'splendour and degeneration ... the culmination of dynastic greatness and the forerunner of an era of deep troubles'.[10] At the Royal Academy, we see only the splendour: extravagant productions in jade, lacquer, porcelain, silk, and enamels. Here are technical tours-de-force, objects in porcelain that simulate wood, pewter, pudding stone. Highly decorative 18th-century objects are shown with their ancient sources of inspiration, as in the

□ 11

□ 12

□ 11. Wang Shimin (1592–1680). *From Scenes Described in Poems of Du Fu,* 1666. One of twelve album leaves, ink and colour on paper. 38.8 x 25.6 cm. The Palace Museum, Beijing

□ 12. Giuseppe Castiglione (Chinese name Lang Shining, 1688–1766). *Spring's Peaceful Message,* c. 1736. Hanging scroll (originally a tieluo painting), ink and colour on silk. 68.8 x 40.6 cm. The Palace Museum, Beijing

□ 13. *Bowl painted with orchids, longevity fungus (lingzhi) and rocks, with a poetic inscription and seals,* Yongzheng period 1723–35. Porcelain with overglaze enamels. Height 5.5 cm. The Palace Museum, Beijing

□ 13

cloisonné bianhu and the Warring States (475–221 BC) bronze original. Qianlong considered one of his most important roles to be the keeper of Chinese culture and preserver of antiquity He studied and collected voraciously, marking the collection with inscriptions and seals whenever he wanted to show his pleasure in an object - and his ownership thereof.

After all this grandeur, it is almost a relief to enter the side gallery of literati paintings. Here, works by Shitao (Zhu Ruoji, 1642–1717), Wu Hong (c.1615 to after 1653) and Gao Xiang (1688–1754), among others, offer a quieter, often soothing view of the world. Some of these artists were 'leftover' subjects, loyal to the Ming, and their works are seen as a form of resistance. Others were professional painters who sometimes worked in the literati style. This gallery makes a lovely exhibition of its own.

China: The Three Emperors, 1662–1795, edited by Evelyn Rawski and Jessica Rawson, with contributions from numerous other leading scholars, is a superb catalogue. It is lavishly illustrated, with thoughtful, detailed entries for all the exhibits and highly informative introductory essays for the eleven sections of the exhibition. There is an extensive public programme at the Royal Academy, including a series of Friday evening lectures; a Focus Day on Imperial Identity in Qing dynasty China; three Monday-afternoon sessions covering Qing Decorative Arts; and a two-day joint symposium, with the School of Oriental and African Studies, on Court Culture under the Qing. This memorable exhibition was sponsored by Goldman Sachs. **MG**

References
1. Rawson J. China: The Three Emperors, 1662–1795: An Exhibition from the Palace Museum, Beijing. *Orientations* Nov/Dec 2005: 46.
2. Naquin S. *The Forbidden City Goes Abroad: Qing History and the Foreign Exhibitions of the Palace Museum, 1974–2004.* Toung Pao 2004, **90**(4-5): 341-397.
3. Dong Qing W. Imperial Genre Painting: Art as Pictorial Record. *Orientations* July/Aug 1995: 18-24.
4. Another of this series is the subject of a short film by David Hockney (A Day on the Grand Canal with the Emperor of China), analysing spatial elements in Chinese painting, which has no single-point perspective. He unrolls the scroll as it would normally be viewed, say, half a metre at a time, rather than all at once, as displayed at the Royal Academy, thus allowing the viewer to change the scenes' boundaries. He contrasts this, first, to the vanishing perspective in a framed Canaletto; then with one of the 12 scrolls recording Qianlong's southern tour.
5. Hearn M. In: Rawski E, Rawson J (eds). *China: The Three Emperors, 1662–1795.* London: Royal Academy of Arts, 2005: 389.
6. Pirazzoli-T'Serstevens M. In: *ibid:* 409.
7. Krahl R. Art in the Yongzheng Period: Legacy of an Eccentric Art Lover. *Orientations* Nov/Dec 2005: 69.
8. Wu Hung S. Emperor's Masquerade – Costume Portaits of Yongzheng and Qianlong. *Orientations* July/Aug 1995: 25-41.
9. Quogiang S. Gentlewomen Paintings of the Wing Palace Ateliers. *Orientations* July/Aug 1995: 56–59.
10. Mote FW. *Imperial China, 900–1800.* Cambridge: Mass and London, 1999: 912–948.

☐ 1

☐ 1. Kaye Donachie. *Epiphany,* 2002. Oil on canvas 36 x 46 cm. Private collection

Tate Triennial 2006:
New British Art

Tate Britain, London

1 March–14 May 2006

In this, the third triennial since the exhibition's inception in 2000, the Tate is once more giving over its galleries to a selection of contemporary art. This year's show expands the number of artists invited to 36, and is curated by Beatrix Ruf, director of the Kunsthalle, Zurich.

The long sweep of the Duveen Galleries has been taken over again, although nothing in it has quite the visual impact of the Jim Lambie/David Batchelor floor and tower combination from 2003's 'Days Like These'. Instead, the North galleries have been turned in to a 'plaza' space for a series of live performances, beginning on the 1 April with Linder's 'The Working Class Goes to Paradise 2000–06' and including a puppet extravaganza by Lali Chetwynd and interventions and performances by Liam Gillick, Pablo Bronstein and Daria Martin, among others.

At the Southern end of the galleries are Rebecca Warren's unfired clay sculptures, crude representations of female bodies reminiscent of Lucio Fontana's lumpy ceramic pieces and full of energy and visual references to Degas and Rodin. 'Fido', for example, marries ruffled ballerina skirts with a prominent bare breast in an accumulation of clumped clay, while 'Come, Helga', with its huge platform shoes from which legs emerge halfway up the calves, tweaks a more modern vision of female sexuality.

'Hostess', meanwhile, towers over the viewer like a piece of religious statuary.

Warren's grotesque figures contrast with the classical lines of three columns by Ian Hamilton Finlay, inscribed with poems that impress the mutability of form on the reader. They allude to Classical myth and ships, two of Finlay's abiding themes. 'Nymph/Ship' reads 'Ships/Nymph/Nymph/Ships/

Bark/Barque/Barque/Bark'. The reference is to Book X of the Aeneid by Virgil, where, as Aeneas' fleet steers to battle in Italy, so in Dryden's translation:

A choir of Nereids meet him on the flood,
Once his own galleys, hewn from Ida's wood;
But now, as many nymphs, the sea they sweep,
As rode, before, tall vessels on the deep.

The way in which sea and wood, and wood and boat are all infused with the same spirit is made manifest by typically economical parallelism and wordplay. The smooth stone columns themselves support this metamorphosis, invoking both trees and masts. Nearby, both thematically and physically, is Cerith Wyn Evans' neon palindrome, a circular Latin inscription hung from the ceiling of the Octagon.

Yet another artist working with text is Liam Gillick, a Triennial veteran. This year he is showing pieces relating to his ongoing project

☐ 2. Peter Doig. *Gasthof,* 2004. Oil on canvas, 275 x 200 cm. Private collection

☐ 3. John Stezaker. *Mask II,* 1991–92. Collage. Courtesy The Artist & The Approach, London

'Construcción de Uno', a fictional story about a group of former factory workers who return to their closed factory and 'improvise new modes of production using redundant factory signage', according to the gallery label. None of this is discernable from the hanging signs that constitute the work, as Gillick has condensed the font until the letters overlap and become almost illegible, instead forming a screen of serifs, lines and holes, a form of sculptural calligraphy cut with precision machinery. It will be interesting to see how his performance, scheduled for the 22 April, relates to this project and his wider interest in bureaucracy and the world of work.

The curators have attempted to find an overriding theme for the third Triennial, and have tentatively come up with the idea that many of the artists focus on the 'reusing and recasting of cultural materials'.[1] This perhaps explains why some of the artists selected are exhibiting work that reaches directly back into the 1970s. Marc Camille Chaimowicz's installation piece 'Here and There ...' (1976–2006) uses three slide projectors and an arrangement of Marcel Breuer armchairs in a shadowy room to create an environment suffused with the past. Images spanning 30 years, slides of the artist in his home, a projected portrait of himself as a young man staring in the mirror and the shadows cast by a vase of wilting flowers and the viewers themselves, all overlap, to create an experience analogous to almost-remembering: the superimposed images remain hermetic and unfamiliar, but recurring shapes and themes seem recognisable.

Another exhibit that evokes a very particular time is Cosey Fanni Tutti's 'Magazine Actions' (1973–80). This reprises the theme of her notorious 'Prostitution'exhibition at the Institute of Contemporary Arts (ICA) in 1976, in which she attempted to show pages from the pornographic magazines in which she was depicted, having entered the sex industry, as she writes in one of the works displayed, 'to create (and purchase) my own image for use as collage material in my work and to gain firsthand experience of being a genuine active participant in the genre'.[2]

We might tell ourselves that society has changed a lot in 30 years and, certainly, the Tate has not felt the need to censor the work as the ICA did in 1976, but increasingly liberal attitudes towards sex and censorship seem to have done little to alter the issues that still make pornography contentious. These, it seems to me, are not questions of obscenity but rather of power, exploitation and an individual's control over their own body and its representation. This is why 'Magazine Actions' retains its power as an experiment in reclaiming what has been sold (a woman's control over her own image) and in using re-contextualisation to overcome fictions created for the purpose of straight male arousal. If there is a question about the work's inclusion it is not over its contemporary relevance, but rather its age, in a show entitled 'New British Art'.

Lucy McKenzie's 'Untitled' (2005) shares this concern for the way in which context frames the reading of sexually explicit material. Her painting depicts an incongruous situation, with

☐ 2

☐ 3

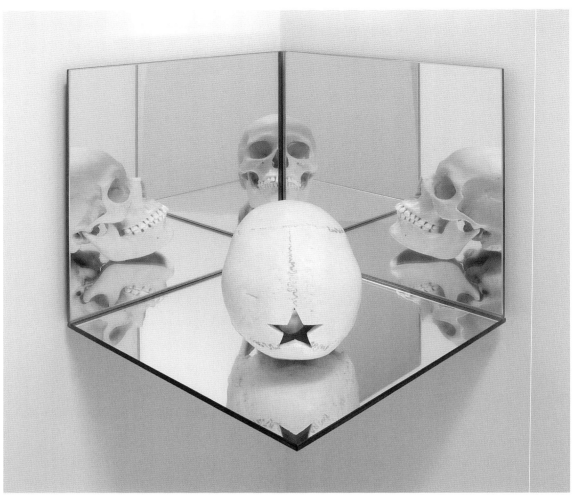

☐ 4

a young woman eating alone in a restaurant, immediately below a large cartoon of a masturbating woman. The fictional narrative this evokes is a labyrinthine story of changing contexts: an erotic cartoon has been found, appropriated and placed in a gallery; the artwork has presumably been bought by a restaurant and hung there; and the imagined juxtaposition thus created has been painted by McKenzie and brought back into the gallery.

Elsewhere, Eva Rothschild's 'Knock Knock' is beautifully simple: a series of branching steel tubes plaited over with leather and hung like a bare inverted tree, the colour of the leather shading from red to black, and the free tassels barely scraping the gallery floor. Its constituent materials of leather and steel, and the relative

simplicity of its construction, link it to the history of industry and craft; its sculptural exploration of space, meanwhile, offsets its totemic associations.

John Stezaker also does unexpected things with minimal materials; in his case, found photographic images. Three pieces from the 'Reparations' series use photos of the aftermath of the storm that devastated South-east England in 1987, adjusting their angle so that the trees and pylons depicted appear miraculously upright - the only problem being that the rest of the world is tipped at a crazy angle. The 'City' series takes small shots of densely built-up urban areas, and inverts them. For the 'Mask' series of collages, Stezaker has superimposed landscape shots − of romantic chasms, waterfalls and caverns - over the faces of film stars from the 1950s. His simple, honed techniques produce arresting results.

Angela Bulloch's 'Disenchanted Forest x 1001' occupies a room of its own: like much of her work, it relies on the mood-altering qualities of light, but also features a kilometre of string tied between a raised floor and suspended ceiling, 1,001 metal discs used by Berlin's environmental agency to number trees, and an ear-splitting electronic soundscape courtesy of Florian Hecker. The overall effect is harsh and discordant − a departure from the gentle minimalism of works such as her 'RGB' spheres, and the glowing 'pixel box' structures whose shifting colours derive from film scenes such as Akira Kurosawa's Ran and Michaelangelo Antonioni's Zabriskie Point. Bulloch's 2005 exhibition at Modern Art Oxford was installed in such a way that these last two pieces ('Fundamental Discord' and 'Z-Point') overlapped and interfered; here, at least the installation has a room to itself, a space in which to create its own environment.

Also worth mentioning is Daria Martin's film 'Wintergarden'; a colourful interpretation of the Persephone myth relocated to the iconic Modernist structure of the De La Warr Pavilion. There are some particularly lovely moments as the Persephone character scales the interior of the pavilion's spiral staircase in an abseil harness, the only sounds the clink of karabiner on steel handrail and her feet slipping on concrete.

Many of the painters at the Triennial have had their work hung together in one corner of the gallery. Of them, Michael Fullerton's two portraits stand out as politically punchy takes on Gainsborough. They owe much to the latter's technique, but subvert the political subtext of 18th-century portraiture by depicting not members of the land-owning classes but Stuart Christie and Beatrice Lyall, an anarchist and a survivor of domestic violence respectively.

Constraints of space mean that no more than a handful of the artists exhibiting at the Triennial can be mentioned here. Not all of the works are especially memorable, and there were points at which I wondered if the Triennial's expansion, from 21 artists in 2000, has not stretched it too far. As Ruf herself says, a Triennial 'cannot provide the same detached, retrospective review of trends and directions in contemporary art as, say, Documenta and the British Art Show, which take place every five years'.[3] It's worth persevering, though, to experience the highlights, including Tino Sehgal's sung intervention 'This is Propaganda', which echoes beautifully through one of the galleries. **JW**

References
1. Ruf B. Revised Narrations. In: Ruf B, Wallis C (eds). *Tate Triennial 2006: New British Art*. London: Tate Publishing, 2006: 10–13.
2. Cosey Fanni Tutti. *Confessions* (extract) 1975–2003.
3. Ruf B. In: *op. cit.*

Royal Academicians in China, 2003–2005

The Sackler Galleries, Royal Academy of Arts, Burlington House, London

23 December 2005–20 January 2006

'Royal Academicians in China, 2003–2005' was conceived to coincide with the Royal Academy's remarkable exhibition, 'China: The Three Emperors, 1662–1795', which presents imperial treasures of the Qing Dynasty. The superb exhibition draws on the collections of the Palace Museum, Beijing, and focuses on the artistic riches of China's last three emperors. It is a spectacular exhibition, and a great credit to the Royal Academy for their organisation of it, and to the team of scholars and curators involved.

The breathtaking effect of the China exhibition perhaps mirrors the impact that a largely unknown culture of contemporary China has had on the Royal Academicians who travelled there between 2003 and 2005, with the generous support of the Red Mansion Foundation. The exhibition was the culmination of a project conceived by the Foundation to promote cultural exchange between the UK and China. The Red Mansion Foundation sponsored a number of Royal Academicians to travel to China to make works inspired by their experiences there. The exhibition was shown at the China National Museum of Fine Arts in Beijing and at the Art Museum in Shanghai in early 2005.

Precipitated by painter John Bellany who, some years ago, related to Nicolette Kwok, founder of the Red Mansion Foundation, how a residency in Mexico in 1996 had inspired him, he expressed his wish to visit China and be further inspired. The idea was consistent with the aim of the Foundation to bring about dialogue between Britain and China. Bellany's desire to visit China was extended to include other artists. The artists were invited to China as part of Red Mansion's ongoing 'Building Bridges' programme. The Foundation chose a further group of academicians: Paul Huxley, Allen Jones, David Mach and Ian McKeever, for their varied approach to art.

John Bellany responded to the visit to China in his typically passionate and effusive manner. There was a hitch at the airport where the massive supply of canvases and paints could not be cleared by customs because it was assumed that such quantities were not for personal use, but for setting up an art materials shop. Eventually cleared by customs and delivered to the hotel rooms where Bellany and his wife were staying, and where John himself was given a studio, he went on to produce a remarkable 48 canvases in just a few weeks. Bellany's work has always been concerned with issues of mortality, for which he has drawn on his upbringing in the Scottish fishing villages of Port Seton and Eyemouth, near Edinburgh. His father was a fisherman and all of his family were intimately involved with the life there.

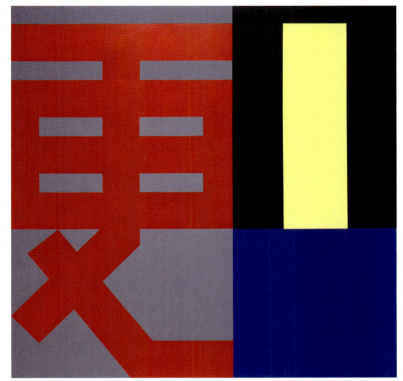

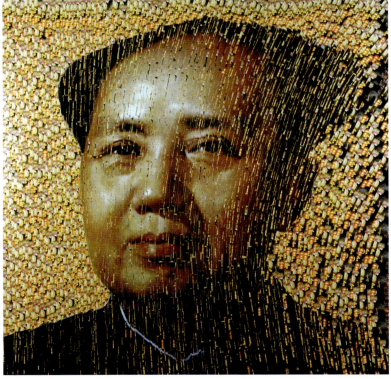

☐ 1

☐ 1. Allen Jones. *Attendant,* 2005. 197 cm, Sculpture.
Image courtesy of The Red Mansion Foundation

☐ 2. Paul Huxley. *Geng,* 2004. 173 x 173 cm, Acrylic on
canvas. Image courtesy of The Red Mansion Foundation

☐ 3. David Mach. *Chairman Mao,* 2004. 183 x 183 cm
Collage. Image courtesy of The Red Mansion Foundation

☐ 3

□ 4

Much of Bellany's work is peopled by strange creatures that derive from mythology, the Bible, Celtic legend, and the mysteries and dangers of the sea. No artist of his generation has made such dramatic, humanistic images. It is interesting to see, when he is placed in a foreign culture, what the impact of that experience has on his work. One of the first features is the fact that Bellany focuses immediately on the sea and boats in Shanghai Harbour, just as he does in Scotland. But, where boats and all aspects of the fishing community in Scotland are steeped in Christian mythology and dogma, no such association in China exists. Bellany is candid in admitting that it will take some time to process this largely intuitive response to his experience there. He chose to portray individuals in their everyday situations, and poignant relationships that he perceived between groups or couples, and within family units. Visually, Bellany found the Chinese sojourn a dramatic and marvellous one. He worked staggeringly long hours: after the mornings spent exploring the city of Shanghai with Helen, he painted from the early afternoon until 4 am. The works in the Royal Academy exhibition were a cohesive group of works of great vitality that continue to inform his work.

The paintings by Paul Huxley could not be more different. In fact, each of the artists on show was represented by works that reflected a sense of personal adventure. Huxley's works made for a spectacular installation along the longest wall in the Sackler Galleries, a space that suited his work extremely well. At first sight, these are masterly formal works that play with the Chinese characters and make a wonderful pattern in sequence. The elegant manner in which Huxley shuffles each colour and shape possesses a simplicity that comes from decades of experimenting with a formal

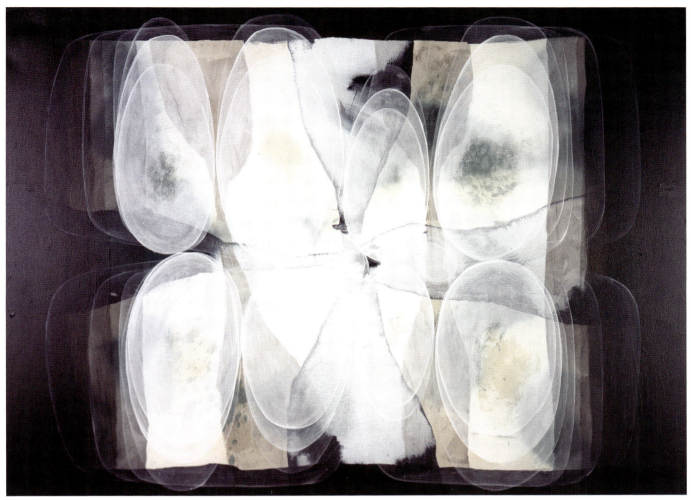

☐ 5

☐ 6

□ 7

□ 8

abstract language. Huxley was one of the young artists in the New Generation annual exhibitions at the Whitechapel Gallery in London, from 1964-68, which sought to represent the latest developments in British contemporary art (other artists included, Bridget Riley, Allen Jones, John Hoyland, Patrick Caulfield and Patrick Proctor). Greatly inspired by the colour field painting of Morris Louis and Kenneth Noland, Huxley has, throughout his career, pursued a personal abstract art. He lived in New York, where the formalism of Clement Greenberg dominated contemporary art. Paul Huxley did not subscribe entirely to such views and maintained a more fluid, ambiguous form of lyrical abstraction. The geometric forms that have long interested Huxley find a playful and musical equivalent in his Chinese works.

Before the proposed trip to China, Huxley had travelled considerably through New York, Hong Kong, East Germany, Cuba and Morocco. He was, therefore, quite used to working in foreign places, yet was reluctant to satisfy the requirements of the Red Mansion project. Huxley was not unfamiliar with the Chinese aesthetic, having lived on the edge of Chinatown in New York, and travelled to Hong Kong, so he was surprised by how dramatically he was affected by the environment in China itself. The degree of commercialisation, the extent of the economic boom and the massive growth in the building of skyscrapers, could not have been in greater contrast to images of communist China that have, until recently, dominated the West's image of China. Unable to read Chinese, but fascinated by the aesthetic of commercial signs in Chinese, which were angular, not fluidly calligraphic, Huxley found the signs exciting. He took notes and photographs (which he does not normally use in his working method), and enjoyed the increased familiarity and recognition of the same. He wanted to use these shapes (words, signs) in compositions, but was mindful of the fact that unless he distorted them, he might make something legible to half the world's population, but not himself.

□ 9

Back in London, Huxley called on a former student from the Royal College, a Chinese artist who was able to translate the words he had collected. Huxley was keen to avoid a situation where the words were meaningless, absurd or obscene. At the same time, he enjoyed the prospect of the symbols or words representing fragments of something seen, culturally out of context, but poetic nonetheless. When Frederick and Nicolette Kwok of the Red Mansion Foundation visited his studio, he had four canvases completed. By chance, they made up part of a very pleasing statement. Kwok asked Huxley if he would consider making a further three to complete a dialogue. When the sequence was completed, they were translated to mean: 'People together make a blue sky even more blue'. The hope for a better world implied in this statement fortuitously expressed the very cultural understanding that the Building Bridges project aimed for. Paul Huxley, like John Bellany, continues to produce images inspired by his Chinese adventure. Huxley has recently made three works that use the images from the Chinese works, but he purposely used red, yellow and blue, in contrast to traditional Chinese art, which did not use colour, and in doing so he is paying tribute to the tenets of Modernism, to Mondrian and Barnett Newman, who celebrated the primary colours in their ground-breaking works.

The project that Huxley was reluctant to take part in has, in fact, prompted the opportunity for a fresh understanding of meaning in abstract art, in a pluralist era. For Huxley's paintings have traditionally involved the division of the canvas into two parts from where one part interacts with the other; and, in turn, the artist interacts with the viewer. The dialogue implicit in Huxley's abstract compositions engages in the exploration of similarities and differences, in a Platonic dialectic, where meaning and understanding are sought. This could not be more appropriate for multicultural societies around the world, in the present troubled times. **JMcK**

Based on interviews with John Bellany and Paul Huxley,
January/February 2006.

□ 1

□ 1. Johan Christian Dahl (1788–1857). *View of Stege in Moonlight,* 1815. © Bergen Art Museum, Norway.

Moonrise Over Europe: JC Dahl and Romantic Landscape

The Barber Institute of Fine Arts, University of Birmingham

20 January–23 April 2006

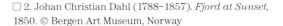
This compact and appealing exhibition is designed to celebrate The Barber Institute's acquisition of Johan Christian Dahl's exquisite moonlit landscape, 'Mother and Child by the Sea'. Dating from 1840, this was probably painted as a memorial to the artist's friend, the great German Romantic landscapist, Caspar David Friedrich, who died that year. An informative and beautifully produced catalogue written by Paul Spencer-Longhurst, senior curator, and published by Philip Wilson Publishers, is available.

When in 1842 the German philosopher Arthur Schopenhauer wrote, 'The moon is sublime and moves us ... because it stays aloof from all our earthly activities, seeing all, yet taking no part in it', he was attempting to define why the earth's silvery night-time companion has held such enigma and allure for mankind, and above all for painters. In an enchanting and varied selection of exhibits, 'Moonrise over Europe' explores northern Romantic artists' preoccupation with the theme of moonlight in the years c. 1770–1860.

Norwegian artist, Dahl (1788–1857), the son of a poor fisherman, quickly outgrew the training facilities available in his homeland, studying instead at Copenhagen and, in 1819, settling in the lively artistic centre of Dresden. A warm and sociable character, he soon met and became friendly with the more introverted and reclusive Friedrich, recording how they once walked together in the park of the Grösser Garten among 'many lovely trees of different kinds, and the moon looked beautiful behind the dark fir trees'.

Friedrich's still, meticulously executed landscapes – products of an art informed by his strict Protestant upbringing and a seeking for the divine in nature – were justifiably famous by the time he and Dahl became acquainted. We are able to see his 'Two Men Contemplating the Moon' (1819), which ranks among his greatest works, and features two *rückfiguren*, or figures, seen from behind, solemnly and companionably gazing at a young sickle moon from the edge of an old forest. 'Greifswald in Moonlight' (1816–17) depicts the artist's birthplace in Pomerania, on the Baltic coast: bathed in an even, gauzy moonlight, the ancient university town assumes an almost ethereal appearance.

Well before their meeting, Dahl had also painted a number of 'moonlights' and, travelling in Europe, he was in the Bay of Naples in 1821 when Mount Vesuvius was active. Here he painted 'Boats on the Beach Near Naples', where fishing crafts lie at anchor in the calm, shimmering waters with the twin peaks of the mountain smoking and flaming behind. Predictably, after his close association with Friedrich began – the two families shared a house in Dresden from 1823 – he was considerably influenced by him, but his own more spontaneous and painterly style soon prevailed. Clients sometimes commissioned pictures from them both, a tranquil coastal scene by Friedrich to pair with a more stormy subject from Dahl.

In the painting now owned by the Barber, Dahl's 'Mother and Child by the Sea', there are echoes of Friedrich's 'Woman by the Sea' (1818). Whereas in Friedrich's work a woman dressed for the windy weather sits idly watching five fishing boats sailing past, in Dahl's picture,

□2

□3

4

5

there seems to be a more personal note, with echoes of his own upbringing in a seafaring community, as the mother and small child eagerly await the return of the little ship from the sea. Among 11 of his works on display are a preparatory sketch and a record drawing for this composition, helping the viewer appreciate his working methods. Dahl also commemorated the magnificent Baroque buildings of his adopted city, and a version of his 'View of Dresden by Moonlight' (1838) has travelled from the National Museum of Art, Architecture and Design in Oslo. This small picture, measuring only 18.5 x 34.5 cm, shows the dome of the Frauenkirche and the tower of the Hofkirche dominating the skyline; silvers and deep blue combine to give it a wonderful jewel-like effect, together with a certain elegiac quality, perhaps indicative of the artist's awareness that his long friendship with Friedrich was nearing an end.

Between 1826 and 1850 Dahl made five journeys to his native Norway, receiving an enthusiastic welcome as a painter of renown. In his late 'Fjord at Sunset' (1850), based on studies made earlier, free and adventurous brush strokes represent the cloud-swept sky and broken surface of the water. Here he has moved far away from the purity and intensity of Friedrich's oeuvre.

Throughout the exhibition, the moon appears in many different guises, gleaming brightly as it emerges from behind rocks; casting a subtle, mysterious light; tossing, on stormy nights, among cloudy seas; or outlined in a slender crescent form. The English artist, Joseph Wright of Derby, achieves considerable drama in his 'A

Moonlight with a Lighthouse, Coast of Tuscany' (c. 1789). As fishermen unload their catch and take down their sail, the moon emerges from behind a lighthouse on a rocky promontory to shine on the oily surface of the water. Two later works look back to a rural, pre-industrial age, when the earth's atmosphere was less polluted: Millet's 'Milkmaid' (c. 1853) employs the glimmering light of a large moon low above the horizon to lend the weary figure a gentle monumentality, while the glorious, gleaming full moon in Samuel Palmer's etching, 'Rising Moon' (1857), reminds us of its once much more significant presence in the night-time sky.

The exhibition benefits from other varied and interesting works, such as the astronomer John Russell's haunting pastel study of a gibbous moon (between half and full moon), made around 1795, which formed part of his own large, topographically detailed map of its surface. Thomas Kerrick's 'Moon Sketchbook', made in charcoal and pastel on blue paper between 1811 and 1818, recorded this Norfolk clergyman's careful observation of the moon in varying conditions and at different phases, pre-dating by more than a decade Constable's sketches of clouds in daytime skies. Fittingly, both German Romantic fascination with the moon and homage to Friedrich's consummately delicate workmanship continue in the final work shown, Arthur Illies' coloured etching 'Ripe Cornfield, Evening' (1896). Here, a slim sickle moon hangs over the waving, finely delineated heads of corn, which is nearing the end of its life and must soon fall to the implements of the harvest. **AK**

Asian Traffic:
Magnetism – Suspension

Zendai Museum of Modern Art, Shanghai

22 October–21 December 2005

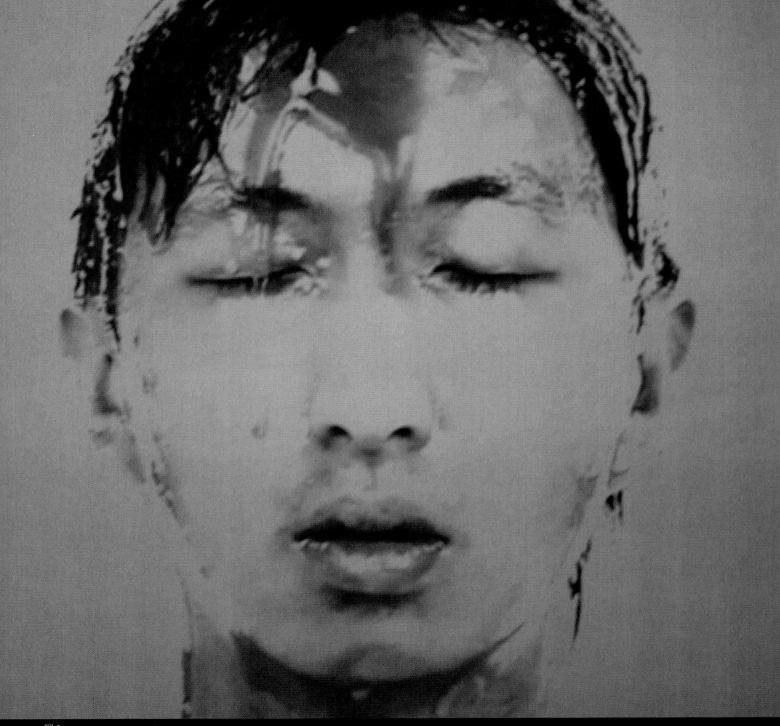

Shanghai is an international city known for its economic prowess and cosmopolitan culture. There is a euphoric sensation in the air. Nothing symbolizes better the lightning speed of development than the Maglev train, which plies the 30-kilometre stretch between Pudong and Shanghai International Airport in a mere eight minutes. Yet, for all the economic achievements, Shanghai is not well known as a centre for the arts. Nevertheless, various individuals and groups are trying to change the scene. The Zendai developer group has set up a Museum of Modern Art in their shopping mall development located in out-flung Pudong. Together with the Asia-Australian Art Centre in Sydney, Australia, they staged an international travelling exhibition there, entitled 'Asian Traffic', and subtitled 'Magnetism – Suspension'.

First shown in Sydney, the exhibition is scheduled to travel to Adelaide, Singapore, Beijing, Shanghai, Shenzhen, Hong Kong, Macau, Tokyo, the United States and Europe. This international touring programme will continue over a period of three years. Featuring 8 artists from Australia and other parts of Asia, this Shanghai exhibition featured a further five local artists in conversation with their foreign counterparts. 'Asian Traffic' seeks to act as a pivotal point to encourage exchanges and investigation in contemporary thinking within and beyond the Asia-Pacific region, in the process, delineating new trajectories in art. Likened to a traffic jam that is so prevalent in any Asian metropolis, where there is an unprecedented rate of information exchange amid an escalating clash of bodies in our contemporary world, this exhibition demonstrated the density and depth of contemporary art produced today.

The words 'magnetism' and 'suspension' encapsulate the current situation in Shanghai exceptionally well. 'Magnetism' in culture implies an irresistible pull of talents to a particular locality. It can also mean a united and integrated Asian perspective. 'Suspension' implies a certain levitation above the profane and mundane. It allows us to distance ourselves in order to feel the presence of Asian problems, as well as finding new ways to solve them. In the Asia-Pacific region, the phenomenon of diaspora cannot be ignored with extensive transnational migration. With this movement of people comes the cross-fertilization of ideas among various distinctive cultures through the process of absorption, reconfiguration, and redistribution of knowledge and technology.

Suzann Victor's installation piece, 'Expense of Spirit in a Waste of Shame', appropriated everyday objects such as light bulbs, mirrors and broken glass in a tense act of mechanistic onanism. The light bulbs flickered on while being lowered to make contact with the mirrors. But which 'infatuated' object is pleasuring which? The work raises questions that pertain to voyeurism, sexual prowess and the status of women in Asia.

Video has also been a popular medium of the artist in their investigations. Young Sydney-based artist, Owen Leong, engages issues of racial and gender identities through his video art work 'Second Skin'. It features a young man

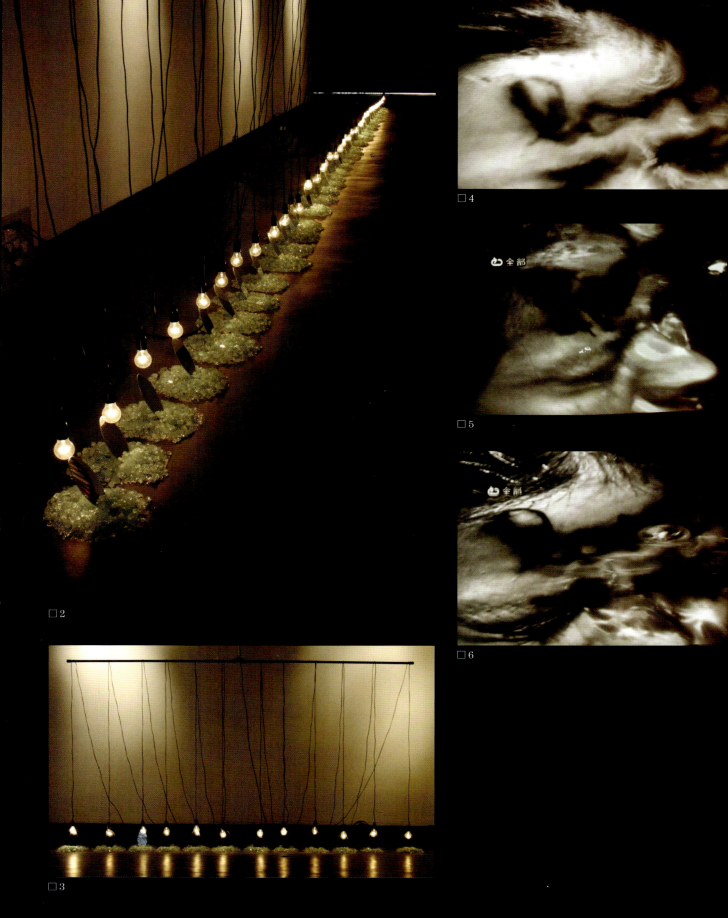

☐ 2

☐ 3

☐ 4

全部

☐ 5

全部

☐ 6

7

8

☐ 9

of Asian origin in a state of distress, with a gluey fluid trickling down his head. The 'self' is used as a metaphor here for the amplification of Asian identities, in a bid to transcend accepted norms and codes pertaining to race, gender and colour. It seeks to infuse images of Asian bodies with new meanings, in the process disrupting conventional hierarchical systems and evincing the invisible power of white hegemony. Leong's work instills spatial anxieties within a sparse interior environment, disarming the audience with a morbid, contorted sense of humour.

Indonesian performance artist, Arahmaiani, provides a social commentary of her native country through the video art work 'Human-Love' (2003). Showing an Asian man exhaling intermittently while being perpetually submerged in water, she explores interpretations of 'humanity' in her native society. Her work draws attention to the view that 'humanity' is an imported Western concept, which is supposed to empower all mankind with equal rights. Yet, when applied in a non-Western context, it tends to marginalize non-Western cultures by positioning it as 'the other'. 'Humanity' became a tool from the West to colonize and dominate economically,

politically and even culturally, the 'primitive' neighbour. Water can give life and yet take life as well.

Chinese artist, Huang Kui, applied highly precise photographs of New York and Shanghai taken by satellites, onto a wall. He then traced the Chinese character 'Dao' (which means streets, roads or the way) in each city, in accordance with the city roads, thereby creating different 'Daos'. Huang's work is charged with a strong influence of Buddhism while he laments the constant addictive tussle between different superpower countries each vying for their own gains. To him, we are merely tiny microbes called mankind that have resided on this planet for only thousands of years. Where are we from? Where are we now? Where are we going?

'Asian Traffic' serves as a focal point for communication and investigations into Asia's conditions and problems. Notions of diaspora and the impact of globalization are reflected not only via the artists' works but also demonstrated through the curatorial concept and method of exhibition. Together, they seek to illustrate the diversity of contemporary Asian culture and thoughts that is in a constant state of evolution. **MCK**

Martin Kippenberger

Tate Modern, London

8 February–14 May 2006

K ippenberger's restless stylistic movements resist the monumentality that a retrospective can impart, and this resistance gives the exhibition a manic energy. Rooms full of painted pastiche spill out into sculptures, books, catalogues and installations; small sketches on hotel notepaper relate obliquely to larger pieces, and internal references bind disparate works together. The curators have drawn inspiration from Kippenberger's own curatorial practices to try to produce a coherent introduction to this prolific artist, who set his life and his art on an equal footing with the claim that 'Every artist is a human being'.

Kippenberger was already upsetting the concept of artist-as-creator with the 1981 pieces that open the show, the series 'Dear Painter, Paint For Me' in which he employed a Berlin sign painter to do the painting for him, turning photos of himself out on the town or reclining on a thrown-away sofa into large, realistic canvases. 'Pale with Envy, He Stands Outside Your Door' was executed in the same year; a series of 21 paintings done in different styles

and a pointed retort to the idea that a bankable signature style is a requisite for success. Yet despite this, it becomes clear - from the collected posters, books, invitations and hoarded ephemera shown in a case in the next room – that Kippenberger was very much a salesman, even describing his life as that of a travelling salesman dealing in ideas.[1]

Such contradictions seem to be present in all of Kippenberger's work: on the one hand, he appropriated art movements, styles and even other artists' work (such as multiples by Joseph Beuys, stuck to his own canvases based on economic graphs), and made extensive use of assistants to attenuate the traditional idea of the artist's role. Yet on the other hand, a strongly anecdotal flavour persists in his work, fostered by the use of jokes and visual or verbal references deeply embedded in private or narrowly historical moments. This turns many of his paintings into rich but confusing riddles, whose original 'answers' can only be teased out with reference to his biography (the construction of which he took a great interest in). Perhaps it is appropriate that

☐ 1. Martin Kippenberger. *One of You, Among You, With You (Einer von Euch, unter Euch, mit Euch),* 1979. 595 x 420 mm. Poster © Estate Martin Kippenberger. Galerie Gisela Capitain, Cologne

☐ 2. Martin Kippenberger. *Martin, Into the Corner, You Should Be Ashamed of Yourself (Martin, ab in die Ecke und schäm Dich),* 1989. Cast resin, pigment, metal, Styrofoam, foam plastic, clothing, 180 x 76 x 30 cm. Collection of Daros Contemporary, Zurich Estate Martin Kippenberger, Galerie Gisela Capitain, Cologne

☐ 3. Martin Kippenberger. *Please Don't Send Me Home (Bitte nicht nach Hause schicken),* 1983. Oil on canvas, 120 x 100 cm. Private Collection © Estate Martin Kippenberger Galerie Gisela Capitain, Cologne

☐ 4. Martin Kippenberger. *The White Paintings of 1991 (Die weissen Bilder von 1991).* Mixed media, 11 parts: 300 x 250cm (3); 240 x 200 cm (2) 180 x 150 cm (2); 120 x 100 cm (1); 90 x 75 cm (3) © Estate Martin Kippenberger. Galerie Gisela Capitain, Cologne

Kippenberger's life seems to attract just as much attention as his art if, as his friend and critic, Diedrich Diederichsen, has claimed, he was indeed a 'Selbstdarsteller' – a self-performer whose notorious antics were an integral part of his oeuvre.[2]

The paintings carried out by Kippenberger himself, whether socialist-realist pastiche or ugly self-portraits in underpants, have an invigorating energy to them, and the humour of the sculpted manikins facing the corner ('Martin, Into the Corner, You Should Be Ashamed of Yourself') do much to win the viewer over. But a few of the pieces on show raise uncomfortable questions about power and its application. Given his oppositional stance to Beuys, who epitomised the idealism of an earlier generation of German artists, Kippenberger's painting of the artist's mother seems to be an unfair gesture of triumph. 'Unfair' is a weak adjective of disapproval, and one I use deliberately to express a certain equivocation. Though I recognise that the distinction between art and life is a blurry one, especially for Kippenberger, Beuys' art would appear to me to be fair game for appropriation just as for criticism, but his family members would not.

I have similar reservations about the last installation in the exhibition, 'Heavy Burschi' ('Heavy Guy'). Kippenberger had an assistant paint collages based on themes from his back catalogue and then, dissatisfied with the result, he destroyed all the assistant's work. Life-size photo reproductions of the assistant's paintings line the walls or are stacked against them, with the trashed paintings in a skip in the middle of the room. This makes a powerful point about employment relations and authorship, but hovers between a constructive drama and a case in which a power inequality is played out for real. By choosing to wield his power as boss or little god, Kippenberger brings the act dangerously close to one of abuse, despite the appearance of photographic technology as the deus ex machina that undoes (or perhaps makes possible?) the violence.

The exhibition's highpoint, however – the installation 'The Happy End of Franz Kafka's "Amerika"' – goes a long way to fulfilling the social promise of Kippenberger's work, his claim that he was 'Einer von Euch, unter Euch, mit Euch' (One of You, Among You, With You). A collection of chairs and tables of vastly disparate provenance and design are set out on a green playing field as if to allow a mass of individual interviews to take place – a reference to the promise of universally fitting employment in Kafka's unfinished novel. With its emphasis on the importance of dialogue and its celebrations of functionalism, reclamation and imagination, this is rightly regarded as one of his major works. **JW**

References
1. Krystof D. The Biggest Theatre in the World: Complexity and Vacuity in 'The Happy End of Franz Kafka's "Amerika"'. In: Morgan J, Krystof D (eds). *Martin Kippenberger.* London: Tate Publishing, 2006: 26–37.
2. Cited by Morgan J Saint Martin. In: *ibid:* 11–22.

□ 2

□ 3

□ 4

☐ 1

☐ 1. Gao Xingjian. *Oblivion,* 86 x 96 cm, 1997.
Private collection

☐ 2. Portrait of Gao Xingjian

The Gao Xingjian Experience:
A Personal Journey to the Infinite

Singapore Art Museum

17 November 2005–7 February 2006

□ 2

'The Gao Xingjian Experience' is the first retrospective art exhibition in Asia of the celebrated multifaceted writer-painter, Gao Xingjian, who was propelled from obscurity to international prominence when he was awarded the Nobel Prize for Literature in 2000. The first Chinese-language Nobel Prize Laureate, who is known for his Modernist and Humanist works of universal validity, Gao is also an eminent artist whose dark, stark, ink paintings highlight the transitory nature of existence. Held from 17 November 2005 to 7 February 2006, the exhibition was organised by the Singapore Art Museum in conjunction with iPRECIATION Gallery. The show featured a total of 60 monochromatic ink paintings, with ten new works from the Paris-based artist. Patricia Ong, Curator of the Gao Xingjian Experience, explains, 'Gao Xingjian regards his paintings as expressions of "inner visions", entry-points to experiencing mindscapes ...' This, perhaps, explains Ong's decision not to place the paintings in chronological order. Instead, she grouped them into three main bodies of works – figurative works, physical interpretations and works dealing with emotion. To complete 'The Gao Xingjian Experience', a bilingual Cultural Forum was held, with discussions by international scholars on Gao Xingjian, including Professor Gilbert Fong of the Chinese University of Hong Kong, Dr Mabel Lee of the University of Sydney, Australia, Dr Noel Dutrait of University of Provence, France, Professor Chen Lusheng of Central Academy of Fine Arts and National Art Museum of China and Dr Quah Sy Ren of Nanyang University, Singapore.

Born in Ganzhou, Jiangxi, China, on 4 January 1940, Gao has survived turbulent changes that occurred in China during the mid-to-late 20th century, including the Japanese invasion of China, the Cultural Revolution, the trauma of a mistaken lung cancer diagnosis, and criticism from the Communist Party during its 'spiritual pollution' campaign. The latter marked the beginning of a self-imposed exile – a 15,000-kilometre journey from Beijing to Sichuan, following the Yangtze from its source to the coast, along the margins of mainstream society. It was a physical and spiritual journey for Gao, in search of the sacred mountain of Lingshan. His travels led him to a greater understanding of his trials, which he subsequently revealed in Soul Mountain, a haunting work of autobiographical fiction.

In 1987, after the government banned his works from publication and performance, Gao left China. He applied for permanent residency in France, and in 1998, he became a French citizen. With the distance from, and removal of, constraints, and the fear of political persecution, Gao's perspective changed. His attitude, adopted over the last 12 years of living in France, can be summarised as 'nothingism'. Essentially, the artist has chosen to disregard any ideologies or trends that would restrict the absolute freedom that he strives for in his work. Attempting to transcend the boundaries of nation and culture, Gao functions as a citizen of the universe, rather than of any particular country. As a result of his all-embracing identity as an artist, it is difficult to label his ink

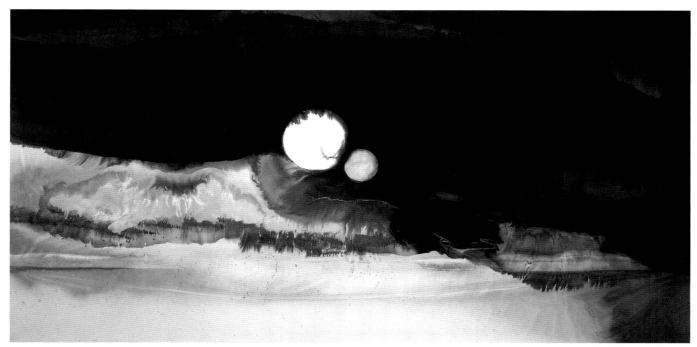

☐ 3

☐ 3. Gao Xingjian. *Eclipse,* 184 x 368 cm, 1999.
Private collection

☐ 4. Gao Xingjian. *Rain of A Beautiful Day,* 144.5 x 139.5
cm, 2005. Private collection

☐ 4

□ 5

□ 6

paintings as Eastern or Western. Dr Gilbert
Fong of the Chinese University of Hong Kong
noted that, like Gao's novels and plays, his
paintings are the products of a 'Chinese eye
looking through a Western lens' and do not
belong to any particular culture.[1]

Apparently, Gao's encounter in 1979 with the
works of European master painters made him
realize that he would not be able to surpass
these masters in the medium of oil. Thus, he
returned to the traditional medium of ink and
brush, and pursued his interest in the speed of
brush and ink on rice paper, and the potential to
be found within the traditional art of Chinese
ink painting. After Gao moved to Paris in 1987,
Chinese ink painting became his main source of

income and gave him the freedom to focus on
creative writing.

One may choose to view Gao's visual art with
expectations based on familiarity with his
written work, or to make connections with his
literature and plays. In Gao's words, from
Return to Painting, 'I would be far happier, in
fact, if you were to simply look at my paintings
without consulting these pages for confirmation
or explanation'.[2] It seems evident that the depth
to be found in Gao's paintings is one visualized
from within the artist. He took up photography
during the Cultural Revolution, and has
incorporated the viewing angle, depth of field
and focus of photography into the landscapes
and narratives of his mind. In 'Soul Mountain'

from Gao's figurative works, the writer-painter's self (or ego) manifests itself as a chaotic mass or black hole with a lone figure. The composition depicts the turmoil and struggles within his innermost thoughts; what Gao sees as, 'More than self-expression ... as a case of self-purification – observing with a pair of somewhat sober eyes the ever-changing world and one's own mainly unconnected self - than an act of self-expression'.[3] Parallels can be found in the novel, Soul Mountain, in which the self manifests itself as the protagonists through the pronouns 'I', 'you', 'she' and 'he'. The novel's intricacies and nuances may seem unfathomable; language fails to bridge the gap between narrative and interior reality. But this is the point at which Gao's paintings begin to tell the story. In 'Oblivion', Gao's depiction of nothingness takes the form of an empty hut accompanied by a single stick-like trunk with a single leaf. This work brings to mind the aesthetics and language of Ni Zan (1306–74), one of the Four Great Masters of the Yuan Dynasty who lived through turbulent dynastic changes. Perhaps the empty hut in Gao's composition, like Ni Zan's empty pavilion, is a representation of Gao's abandoned home and the end of his idealistic view of the world into which he was born. The single trunk standing alone in the barren composition of In the Rain resonates with the same hidden declaration of survival in a hostile world.[4]

A quiet moment spent viewing Gao's monochromatic ink paintings in an empty gallery is like an intimate conversation with the writer-painter, who is baring his soul. If you expect to emerge from the experience of viewing this work with a greater awareness of the riddles of life, you might be disappointed. However, do not be surprised if you come out a little shaken from the intensity and feeling humbled by the encounter. Kwok Kian Chow, Director of the Singapore Art Museum, compares the experience to that of sudden enlightenment in Chan (Zen) philosophy, with the paintings capturing a heightened moment of human existence. The compelling narratives in black and white tones express the intellect and emotive power of the painter's unique language, creating a surreal watercolour-like image in ink.
HK

References
1. Xingjian G. *EXPERIENCE Programme: Bilingual Cultural Forum,* 20 November 2005.
2. Xingjian G. *Return to Painting.* New York: HarperCollins, 1999.
3. Xingjian G. *Thoughts on Painting.* Paris, 14 July 1995.
4. Imperial China's Splendors, 12 July 1996 transcript.

On the trail of wise fools and simpletons in the Himalayas

Holy Madness: Portraits of Tantric Siddhas

The Rubin Museum of Art, New York

10 February–4 September 2006

Those unfamiliar with Tantric Siddhas and Himalayan art, culture and religion may be surprised to learn that Himalayan history is filled with stories of spiritual beings who, it is said, attained enlightenment through highly unorthodox means. 'Holy Madness: Portraits of Tantric Siddhas', currently on view at New York's Rubin Museum of Art, presents more than 100 paintings, sculptures and photographs of Tantric Siddhas, produced during these figures' illustrious history. Known as saintly tricksters who renounced accepted beliefs, opinions and behaviours to accelerate their spiritual progress, the early masters were responsible for transmitting Tantric Buddhism from India to the Himalayas between the seventh and 11th centuries.

The word 'Siddha' refers to a spiritually accomplished being. The great masters are known as Mahasiddhas. They lived in India, Sri Lanka and Malaysia, practising Tantra, an esoteric form of Buddhism. Tantrikas believe that enlightenment can be attained in one lifetime, rather than over the course of many, and that any pursuit, occupation or behaviour may serve to open the gates of consciousness. Their belief led some Tantrikas to a variety of pursuits and behaviour - from the most common to the most outlandish - all in the service of awakening. The tradition of noble, charismatic ascetics, who wander penniless through the country, often taking students, continues today. While the many rituals associated with Trantra have changed, or been softened, Tantrikas still embrace chanting, meditating on mandalas and sexual symbolism in which sun (shiva) and moon (shakti) are united. Their practices could include some or all of the four main forms of yoga: Karma yoga (good works); Bhakti yoga (the yoga of devotion); Jnana yoga, (the yoga of knowledge); and Raja yoga (physical and mental

☐ 1. *Drenpa Namka*. Tibet, 15th century. Metalwork. Rubin Museum of Art, C2003.31.1 (HAR 65183)

☐ 2. *Avadhutipa*. Tibet, c. 17th–18th century. Gilt metalwork with turquoise inlay. Rubin Museum of Art, C2005.8.2 (HAR 65408)

☐ 3. *Krsnapa*. Tibet, 16th–17th century. Gilt copper. Rubin Museum of Art, C2005.16.54 (HAR 65477)

☐ 4. *Jalanadhara*. Tibet, c. 16th century. Metalwork with pigment. Rubin Museum of Art, C2003.13.4 (HAR 65218)

□ 1

□ 2

□ 3

□ 4

century, shows eight Siddhas on the exterior of the lotus leaves, while eight female Yoginis appear on the interior of the leaves. As an object of devotion, the piece offers much to contemplate, but as a visual form apart from its function, the work is remarkable.

Scholars have noted a striking similarity between early Hindu (Indian) Siddha imagery and later Tibetan depictions. Most notable, perhaps, are hairstyle (coiled in a prominent mass on top of the head); long moustaches and beards; elongated earlobes from which hang elaborate earrings; and symbols marking the third eye point between a Siddha's arching brows.

Photography is well represented in the main body of the exhibit. 'A Holy Man, Kathmandu, Nepal', 1985, by Rosalind Solomon (silver gelatin print) helps to connect the iconoclasts of the distant past to the Tantrikas of today. The figure exhibits the hallmarks of the wandering ascetic: nearly naked body decorated with necklaces and armlets; tangled hair; face marked with ashes and the ubiquitous third eye-point symbol; and eyes closed in contemplation of the infinite. As in all works of devotional art, the subject of the photograph contributes as much to the quality of the image as the artist who created it.

In addition, visitors can view two photographic exhibits, 'Mahasiddhas at Gyantse' features Ulrich von Schroeder's photographs of 15th-century murals of Tibetan Mahasiddhas, the first time the murals have been exhibited or published as a complete cycle; and 'Mahasiddhas at Alchi', a collage of photographs by Jaroslav Poncar. The sections of Poncar's collage combine to form a nearly life-size image of a giant standing bodhisattva formed in clay. Created from the late 12th to early 13th centuries, the sculpture is most notable for the bodhisattva's skirts, which are covered with miniature paintings of a set of the 84 Mahasiddhas.

After an initial viewing of 'Holy Madness', visitors will have a good understanding of the visual conventions used by the nameless artists who created the works, and the role played by these pieces in Tantric practice - but repeated viewings will likely prove rewarding: the images were meant to deepen aspirants' intuitive understanding through devotion and meditation. The curator and museum staff have done a splendid job of creating a meditative atmosphere in which one can view the works on a visual level, appreciating the range of dynamic colouration and composition, consider the figures' legends and legacy and contemplate their symbolic meaning.

The exhibition catalogue, Holy Madness: Portraits of Tantric Siddhas, edited by Rob Linrothe, Associate Professor of Art History at Skidmore College in Pennsylvania (Rubin Museum of Art, 2006), is a beautifully produced 450-page, four-colour volume that presents a comprehensive overview of the colourful characters, mythology and symbolism of Himalayan art, culture and religion. **CDM**

☐ 1

☐ 2

☐ 3

☐ 4

□ 5

□ 6

□ 5. *Kamala. Suvarnadvipa, Viraya*, Tibet, c. 17th century. Mineral pigments on cloth.
Rubin Museum of Art, C2004.14.2 (HAR 65349)

□ 6. *Virupa, Krsnapa, Damarupa, and Avadhutipa*. Tibet, 17th century. Mineral pigments on cloth 25 x 20 in.
Rubin Museum of Art, C2002.45.2 (HAR 65377)

control). Raja yoga is considered to be the most profound, or 'royal' road to yoga.

Curated by Kathryn Selig Brown, 'Holy Madness' opened on 10 February and runs until 4 September 2006. Located in the former Barneys New York building on Seventh Avenue, a longtime cultural icon, the museum was inaugurated in the fall of 2004. During a period of more than five years, the building was transformed into a calm retreat from New York's hustle and bustle. Mirroring the artistic content contained within, the decor invites a slower pace and contemplation.

Before making their way up the central spiral staircase to the top two floors, on which the exhibit is staged, visitors can walk through the museum's introduction to Himalayan art on the second floor. Here, brick- and sage-coloured walls provide an introspective background. The orientation to Himalayan art – where, how and why it is made, its function and symbolism – provided by the introduction is a good preface to the legends viewers will read about in the 'Holy Madness' exhibit labels.

Commissioned by powerful rulers and religious figures, many portraits of the Siddhas were created as part of a series of devotional visual texts, while others are single representations of a master. Some elicit a light, joyful response, while others have a more somber tone. For example, Savaripa and Darikapa (The Hunter and the Slave of a Temple Dancer), painted in eastern Tibet, circa 1600, on cloth with mineral pigments, depicts a bi-level scene: Savaripa the Hunter appears above with a bodhisattva, or compassionate being, who has shown him the error of killing animals. Full of remorse, Savaripa is said to have turned his life over to Tantric meditation. The artist has shown Savaripa in his other form, Wearer of the Peacock Plume, in a feathered cape, pointing toward an escaping deer. Darikapa is shown in the lower part of the cloth panel. This figure renounced his kingdom to follow Luipa, the Fish-Gut Eater, a spiritual master. At some point, Darikapa was sold to the main temple dancer. He remained her slave for 12 years. When she heard him discourse on Tantric philosophy, Darikapa's mistress embraced Tantra and became his disciple.

Heavily laden with symbolism - much of it obscure until one knows the legends surrounding the Siddhas – the portraits are intriguing character studies. From Virupa the Ugly One and Damarupa the Drum Holder to Jalandhara the Net Holder and Tilopa the Sesame Seed Pounder, the stories are captivating. For instance, a copper figure of Tilopa from 16th-century Tibet shows a Siddha said to have achieved enlightenment while pounding sesame seeds. During the day, Tilopa spent his time pounding seeds, but during the evenings he worked as a prostitute's pimp. Are the pursuits in conflict? Tantrikas would say no, as everything here on earth can serve the higher purpose of spiritual enlightenment.

Aside from legendary and mythological connections, many of the works stand as examples of the artists' masterful handling of their materials: the sensuous sculptural form of a three-dimensional lotus-shaped copper mandala, made in eastern India during the 12th century, shows eight Siddhas on the exterior of the lotus leaves, while eight female Yoginis appear on the interior of the leaves. As an object of devotion, the piece offers much to contemplate, but as a visual form apart from its function, the work is remarkable.

Scholars have noted a striking similarity between early Hindu (Indian) Siddha imagery and later Tibetan depictions. Most notable, perhaps, are hairstyle (coiled in a prominent mass on top of the head); long moustaches and beards; elongated earlobes from which hang elaborate earrings; and symbols marking the third eye point between a Siddha's arching brows.

Photography is well represented in the main body of the exhibit. 'A Holy Man, Kathmandu, Nepal', 1985, by Rosalind Solomon (silver gelatin print) helps to connect the iconoclasts of the distant past to the Tantrikas of today. The figure exhibits the hallmarks of the wandering ascetic: nearly naked body decorated with necklaces and armlets; tangled hair; face marked with ashes and the ubiquitous third eye-point symbol; and eyes closed in contemplation of the infinite. As in all works of devotional art, the subject of the photograph contributes as much to the quality of the image as the artist who created it.

In addition, visitors can view two photographic exhibits, 'Mahasiddhas at Gyantse' features Ulrich von Schroeder's photographs of 15th-century murals of Tibetan Mahasiddhas, the first time the murals have been exhibited or published as a complete cycle; and 'Mahasiddhas at Alchi', a collage of photographs by Jaroslav

Poncar. The sections of Poncar's collage combine to form a nearly life-size image of a giant standing bodhisattva formed in clay. Created from the late 12th to early 13th centuries, the sculpture is most notable for the bodhisattva's skirts, which are covered with miniature paintings of a set of the 84 Mahasiddhas.

After an initial viewing of 'Holy Madness', visitors will have a good understanding of the visual conventions used by the nameless artists who created the works, and the role played by these pieces in Tantric practice - but repeated viewings will likely prove rewarding: the images were meant to deepen aspirants' intuitive understanding through devotion and meditation. The curator and museum staff have done a splendid job of creating a meditative atmosphere in which one can view the works on a visual level, appreciating the range of dynamic colouration and composition, consider the figures' legends and legacy and contemplate their symbolic meaning.

The exhibition catalogue, Holy Madness: Portraits of Tantric Siddhas, edited by Rob Linrothe, Associate Professor of Art History at Skidmore College in Pennsylvania (Rubin Museum of Art, 2006), is a beautifully produced 450-page, four-colour volume that presents a comprehensive overview of the colourful characters, mythology and symbolism of Himalayan art, culture and religion. **CDM**

□ 7

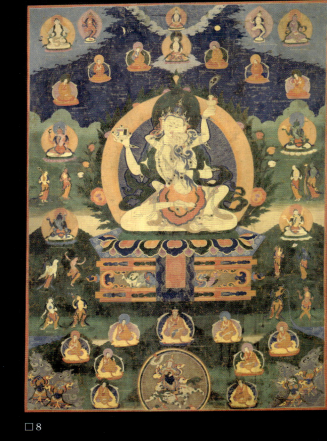

□ 8

□ 9

□ 10

Gothic Nightmares: Fuseli, Blake and the Romantic Imagination

Tate Britain, London

15 February–1 May 2006

What fascinates us in an artwork? One answer to this question is content that conveys a sense of harmony and rightness: summer landscapes bathed in sunshine; human beauty, strength and agility; stories that show compassion and virtue rewarded; all things that please, reassure and comfort us with life-affirming visions of the world. But this is not all. How else do we explain the enduring popularity of ghost stories, horror films, human monsters and 'The Silence of the Lambs'? We have to admit to a corresponding fascination for the ugly, the destructive and the macabre, resulting in extreme cases of what Ruskin famously called 'an insane and wolf-like gloating over the garbage of death'.

During the period 1770–1830, British culture became preoccupied with a curious range of such themes. They featured frightening or horrific subjects, such as ghosts, witches, phantoms and malign manifestations of the supernatural. They also included subjects that, although not malign, were regarded as overwhelming or awesome, such as volcanoes, storms, waterfalls, and concepts such as astronomical infinity. In critical terminology, these themes became loosely grouped in a category referred to as 'the sublime'. 'The beautiful' in art and nature left one with a

feeling of pleasure, satisfaction and fulfilment; the sublime, on the other hand, often evoked feelings of unease, awe, fear or revulsion; and yet one felt an 'agreeable horror' in their contemplation.

The broad area of the sublime may be subdivided into, on the one hand, naturally occurring phenomena such as volcanoes and storms, which are awesome without human intervention; and on the other, those things that may be said to arise from human action or the human psyche: phantoms, witches, goblins, extreme evil and the destructive forces of human passion. This exhibition explores the latter phenomenon with particular reference to the work of three close contemporaries: Fuseli, Blake and Gillray.

Fuseli was one of those remarkable émigrés whom Britain has so willingly taken to its bosom, and who then went on to become a major formative influence upon British culture. He was Swiss by birth and settled in London after a period of study in Italy. He became a figure of major importance in British art and art education, becoming a member of the Royal Academy and, subsequently, Professor of Painting and Keeper. As such, and through his extensive writings on art, he exerted continuing influence on a generation of British artists as

□ 1

□ 1. Henry Fuseli. *The Nightmare,* 1781. Oil on canvas, 127 x 102 cm. Detroit Institute of the Arts

superficially remote from his own tastes as Turner and Constable.

Fuseli's painting 'The Nightmare' dominates the exhibition. A beautiful, lightly clad girl lies prostrate on a bed or couch. Her arms hang lifelessly, with her fingers resting limply on the floor. Her eyes are closed and her mouth falls open. Her golden hair cascades down behind her. Her bosom heaves beneath a scanty chemise. Perched grimly upon her stomach is a hunched semi-human gargoyle of a being, which glares at the spectator with an expression of gloating satisfaction. A sightless horse, the proverbial 'nightmare' thrusts its grotesque head between the curtains surrounding the scene, paradoxically a blind witness to this macabre event.

The image brings together many of the recurrent preoccupations of what became known as the Gothic. It evokes a threatening and anomalous being, having some human attributes, but not fully human; it juxtaposes ravishing beauty with grotesque ugliness; it takes place in the domain of night and sleep, when reason and clarity recede and we become vulnerable to the forces of darkness; it generates a sense of impending disaster.

In the art and culture of the late 18th and early 19th centuries, we find two powerful yet contradictory forces. On the one hand, there are the fruits of the Enlightenment, and the exercise of reason in the achievements of science, technology and philosophy, creating a vision that gave hope for the realisation of utopia. On the other hand, we find a strengthening and deepening of interest in all those human traits that militate against reason: the irrational, the nightmare, spectres, violence and the grotesque. In that age, these flights of the imagination did not appear to be susceptible to reason and logic. They did not fit into any scientific system of enquiry or understanding. It was not until a century later, with the development of psychology and the birth of psychoanalysis, that we find any empirical and scientific system attempting to cope with them.

Artists with a taste for the Gothic ransacked art, literature and history for suitable subjects. Of particular interest were obscure periods of medieval history, Shakespeare's supernatural themes, such as those in Macbeth, folklore and the Old Testament. This journey into the unknown often led to very basic themes that appeared to unify this otherwise disparate subject matter. There were dark, powerful forces at play, over which we have little control. They burst forth in acts of terrible violence and brutality. Sex played a prominent role here, as a force that was not completely subject to social or rational control and could break out with terrible destructive force upon personal lives and social arrangements.

The theme of sexuality, which features so prominently, resulted in imagery that is both powerful and explicit. These images are not 'erotic' in the sense of arousing pleasurable admiration or wonder; nor are they 'pornographic' in the modern sense of degraded erotic imagery of no intrinsic merit intended to do no more than arouse or stimulate sexual appetite. The preoccupation with sexuality is visible, albeit in a literally veiled form, in a painting like 'The Nightmare'. It is more rampant and explicit in other images, not only in the high art of Fuseli and his circle, but in the caricature images of popular prints which fed upon it, such as those of Gillray. It is not surprising that the Victorian public later came to find much of the art of this period disturbing or obscene, leading Ruskin, as Turner's executor, to destroy an unknown number of his drawings in the genre.

The theme of the breakdown of social order resulting in violence and brutality led artists back to classical and medieval themes with those ingredients. We have to remind ourselves that the artists of the period lived through one of the most threatening and turbulent periods in history. For more than two decades, Europe was thrown into the turmoil of the French Revolution, which soon spilt over into the wars and territorial ambitions of France. The old social and political orders, with all their faults, often crumbled away leaving nothing but chaos and destruction.

One question I always ask myself on visiting an exhibition is whether I would like to own or live with any of the work presented. In this case, I must confess that there was little to which I could give an unhesitating affirmative. Although much of the work is 'interesting' – a word detested by many artists – there was little to warm the cockles of an aesthete's heart. Many of the exhibits could be described as powerful, dynamic and inspired, but much was equally repellent and disturbing. Fuseli's large subject pictures draw heavily upon his time in Rome, with exaggerated reminiscences of

Michelangelo and the Manieri. Over-musculated figures strut and strain as they emerge from the pervasive gloom of the canvas. Blake similarly coined a fanciful and exaggerated anatomy of his own, which seems to bear very little resemblance to Gray's.

The dark forces that so preoccupied the artists of the period remain vividly with us today. Popular literature and film constantly dwell upon the supernatural, the perverted and the destructive. Sex continues to have the power to destroy lives, to bring down politicians and, indeed, governments. On the day I visited the exhibition – 10 March 2006 – the lead item on the news was the death of Profumo. His story epitomises the perennial destructive power of sexual appetite. At almost half a century after the event, the thing we remember when all else is forgotten is this inexorable force and its consequences. The newspaper placard at the exit from Pimlico station on my way to the Tate proclaimed simply, 'SEX SCANDAL MINISTER DEAD'. This is the epitaph by which he will be remembered. Perhaps a tragic and suitable theme for a Gothic artist. **CA**

Exiles and Emigrants: Epic Journeys to Australia in the Victorian Era

National Gallery of Victoria, Melbourne

9 December 2005–26 March 2006

National Museum of Australia, Canberra

21 April–4 June 2006

☐ 1. Ford Madox Brown. *The Last of England,* 1855. Oil on wood panel, 82.6 x 75.0 cm. Birmingham Museum and Art Gallery, Birmingham. Purchased 1891

□ 1

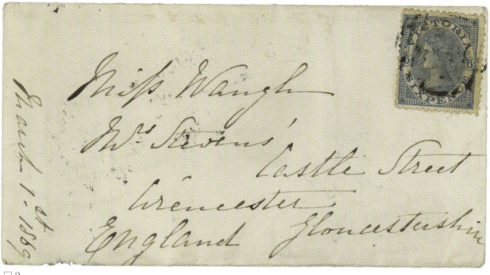

□ 2

The exhibition 'Exiles and Emigrants: Epic Journeys to Australia in the Victorian Era' has succeeded in seizing the imagination of thousands of visitors who have responded to the stories depicted in these Victorian narrative paintings. For most viewers, particularly in a nation settled by immigrants (primarily convicts in the initial, enforced settlement of New South Wales), each story recalls those of their own forbears. Prompted by the writing materials located at the conclusion of the exhibition, many have been encouraged to document their own individual histories: these are now pinned up on the final wall. Showing the universality and continuing relevance of immigration, the National Gallery of Victoria (NGV) curators have incorporated a contemporary work from their collection at the conclusion of this 19th-century survey – Jan Nelson's 'International Behaviour' (2000), which starkly depicts the recent arrival of boat people to these shores.

The guest curator, Patricia Tryon MacDonald, herself an emigrant to Australia, has an innate sympathy for the complex feelings of the subjects of these images. She has hung the exhibition in a clear progression, moving from the motivations behind the departure, through the dangers and boredom of the journey, to the arrival in a new land, the exchange of letters between the new settlers and those back 'home' and finally, the pioneer's experience. As MacDonald stresses: 'It is a story of people – human beings: where they went and why they went, and what they faced up to. They were astonishing people with great courage'.

The paintings in the first room help to explain just why around 15 million emigrants left the United Kingdom in the Victorian era. During this period, while industrialisation created great wealth and opportunity for many in Britain, others lost their traditional livelihoods. The title of this sector is borrowed from Ford Madox Brown's icon of English emigration, 'The Last of England' (1855), which easily dominates the gallery with its clear, luminous pre-Raphaelite palette. Patricia MacDonald rightly saw this as the key to the exhibition: 'When you are putting together an exhibition that has never ever been done before and are trying to tell a story, you are only as good as the loans you can get'. Never lent outside England before, this is the first time it has hung beside its Scottish counterpart, Thomas Faed's 'The Last of the Clan' (1865). This work from the NGV's collection, graphically illustrates the desolation caused by the Highland

2. Unknown. Envelope from Victoria to UK, 1st March 1869. 6.8 x 12.1 cm (envelope). Private collection, Victoria

3. James Tissot (France 1836–1902, lived in England 1871–82). *The Emigrants,* 1873. Oil on wood panel, 39.4 x 17.8 cm. Private collection, Los Angeles. Photograph courtesy of Kings Galleries Corp., USA

clearances and the mid-century potato famine, by showing the clans reduced to one old man and a young girl. Ford Madox Brown's renowned work was painted over three years, at a time of personal conflict for the artist. It captures the contradictory feelings of the young family - their apprehension and sense of loss alongside their strength and optimism, in what the artist described as, 'the circle of love' (expressed by the father, mother and child, and their linked hands). In the exhibition, one also finds less well-known works from the outer circle of pre-Raphaelitism, such as Henry Wallis's 'The Stonebreaker' (1857), in which the artist's striking depiction of evening light bathes a dead worker's body in an unearthly glow. Both works are generously lent by the Birmingham Museums and Art Gallery, who, according to MacDonald, agreed to send the works to Australia because, 'this is the first time anybody has really tackled the subject [of emigration]'. Another powerful image, rarely seen by the broader public, is Lady Butler's 'Evicted' (1890), in which the Irish peasant woman stands barefoot and proud in the still smoking ruins of her destroyed home. Painted when England was preventing Irish home rule, it was an unpopular depiction there, for an Ireland already in revolt.

3

4

After the opening section – with its group of impressive social realist pictures – there follows a series of themed alcoves that focus on particular aspects of the emigrant's departure and journey. One section named 'The Final Farewell', for instance, addresses the moment of departure, and one is struck here by the importance of the written word in shaping the Victorian public's understanding of this phenomenon. Charles Dickens' vivid description of the departing emigrant ship in David Copperfield is shown to have directly influenced Henry Nelson O'Neil's 'The Parting Cheer' (1861). The work of the 18th-century poet, Oliver Goldsmith, inspired three other works – Richard Redgrave's 'The Emigrant's Last Sight of Home' (1858), Joseph Severn's 'The Deserted Village' (1857) and Thomas Falcon Marshall's 'Emigration – the Parting Day' (1852). Other aspects of the emigrant's experience follow: 'Women and Children Last' where Frank Holl's painting 'Gone!' (c.1887) clearly demonstrates the plight of the women and children left behind; 'The Voyage', where displayed objects augment the images of shipboard experience, ranging from sketching, shipboard games and quilt-making to braving the perils of shipwreck; then 'The Arrival'; 'From a Distant Land' and finally 'The Pioneer'. In the section, 'From a Distant Land', an intriguing trilogy of images can be found: Harden Sidney Melville's work entitled 'The Squatter's Hut: News from Home' (1850–51); Thomas Webster's 'A Letter from the Colonies' (1852) and David Davies' 'From a Distant Land' (1889). These paintings display the importance of maintaining links with Britain through letters. Today's children, accustomed to the immediacy of electronic communications, have been intrigued to recognise the importance of handwriting; a nearby display cabinet containing a number of 19th-century letters with their minutely crossed writing and complex addresses reinforces the theme.

By the exhibition's end, the overwhelming impression is one consumed by nostalgia and loss. The selection of paintings, photographs, documents and objects emphasise the human face of these epic journeys – forced departures, dangerous voyages and homesickness. The figure of the successful adventurer happily seeking his fortune abroad is singularly absent from the gallery walls. Even the last painting, Frederick McCubbin's great hymn to Australian settlement, entitled 'The Pioneer' (1904), recounts a tale of endurance and hard work in a very foreign land. This exhibition forces us to remember that one in six of Queen Victoria's subjects was compelled to leave Britain in small boats. And this is the exhibition's strength: through the works selected, countless ballads of individual frailties and courage are sung, capturing the imaginations of the thousands of visitors who have come, looked, and felt impelled to write their own stories. **BBK**

☐ 1

☐ 1. Jon Schueler. *My Garden is the Sea, Mallaig Vaig,*
1957. 72 x 60 in (o/c 57-30). © Jon Schueler Estate

Jon Schueler: a painter of our time

Jon Scheuler (1916–1992): Time Has Three Suns

ACA Galleries, New York

21 January–18 February 2006

Jon Scheuler: Five Decades

Ingleby Gallery, Edinburgh

26 January–11 March 2006

The American Expressionist painter Jon Schueler (1916–92) was recently the subject of growing interest on both sides of the Atlantic. When he died in New York City in August 1992, aged 75, he had a considerable following, which recalled his status in the 1950s and 1970s. For a significant period, he was one of Leo Castelli's stable, showing important early exhibitions there in 1957 and again in 1959. In fact, Schueler comprised the first one-man show at Castelli's new 4 East 77th Street gallery. Critics, however, invariably misinterpreted his work, for example, *Life* Magazine (December 2, 1957) proposed that Schueler was one of a new generation of painters inspired by the work of the once-scorned painter Claude Monet. Schueler was no doubt glad of such publicity, but he would surely have preferred to have been linked art historically with JMW Turner. Schueler often referred to Turner's vision, and his encounter with the massive body of Turner's work at the British Museum (19,300 works) in London was pivotal:

When I saw the Turners through the years and compared them with other work, it seemed to me that he went further into nature and further into the sensation of nature in paint than any other painter. He, the stylist of incredible facility, did the most to break down style, to destroy it, to find the possibility of paint talking as paint, as an extension of the most immediate perception and sensibility, so that it became most like nature. This is what I would like my paintings to be.[1]

A compelling photograph of Schueler, in *Life,* in front of a key work of the 1950s, 'The Lake', showed him in the role as artist as celebrity, a role that an artist of Schueler's sensibility found impossible to maintain.

Jon Schueler was a voracious reader (he particularly admired the Australian author Patrick White). He was also an accomplished and skilful letter writer and diarist. Castelli included Schueler's 'In the Wild Garden' in a show in November 1957. The curator and art historian JH Baur, in New York as Director of the Whitney Museum of American Art, included Schueler in his key exhibition there. He also described Schueler's work in the accompanying catalogue, in his seminal article entitled 'Nature in Abstraction: The Relation of Abstract Painting and Sculpture to Nature in Twentieth-Century American Art'. Later in 1975, Baur organised a show of Schueler's work at the Whitney. In terms of recognition, Schueler's work received positive press, notably in *The New York Times* (20 November 1957) when he was only 41; it was pivotal to his career. But, true to his nature, Jon Schueler was already absent from the very scene and recognition that most artists would have aspired to. Indeed, Schueler travelled, that autumn, to the remote and unlikely destination of Mallaig, a tiny village in western Scotland. Castelli and others had to contact him via a manual telephone exchange, on the remote Scottish coastline. Later, in July 1959, Schueler reflected on the significance of this move:

I went to Scotland to think about [death] along with everything else. I wanted to watch the Devil come to me there. I felt that I could face him more surely and recognise him for what he is. The city is too full, perhaps too full of wonderful things, wonderful temptations disguised as necessities, too full of necessities disguised as life. I wanted to go to the mountain and to meet my own thoughts, and to meet God and to meet the Devil and see his face and tell him to go to Hell. The confusion of my life had been yearly compounded for 40 years. A north wind blowing off the sea promised clarity. I wanted to live in the middle of one of my paintings for a year. I wanted to be in one spot and watch the painting change. I saw clouds menacing my mind's eye, and the rain shafts of the mist obliterating horizons and forming new forms with the clouds and landmasses blending with the sea. I chose northern Scotland as my cathedral, because for my needs at that moment, it seemed the only church that would do.[2]

As interest in his work was humming in Manhattan, Schueler leased a cottage in Mallaig for the winter months and through to the spring. In doing so, he took a lease also on the immeasurable solitude of the place, and the compelling beauty of the surrounding skies, in the winter dark. Back in New York, Castelli had been mostly successful, selling work both there and to Germany. In Mallaig, Schueler recorded his feeling of desolation, not always inspired by the long nights and wild weather. There he worked relentlessly, and by March 1958 could dispatch no less than 45 paintings from Scotland to Castelli. Exhausted, he then moved on to work for a while in Paris. Paintings done in Mallaig have a dramatic force but this lyrical quality is still sustained in the works from France, calmer and less powerful. While in France recently, the author and critic Diane Cousineau managed to track down an important work, which Schueler had executed for the community of Les Prêtres Passionistes at Clamart in 1958, before departing. This superb and greatly treasured painting now hangs in the parish hall of St Lez - St Giles, Thiais. It testifies particularly to the spirituality in Schueler's work, and it might be said, therefore, in his mind.

□ 2

Jon Schueler had said at the time, in a letter to Castelli, 'I have no telephone, but there is a Passioniste order of priests across the way – they are good friends of mine – have a telephone – and will take a message for me. I have just finished a large painting, which I painted for their chapel. It is about the Passion and Resurrection of Christ, and will hang above the altar (this is a gift, of course)'.

When he planned to return to New York at the end of 1958, as his friends warned him, the enthusiasm that had developed in the previous year had already waned. Castelli did his best to put a good light on the situation, telling him that he had sold no less than four more paintings. Schueler himself observed that, 'the safest place to paint was New York, but there are no snow clouds'. Despite some misunderstandings over prices of paintings of a genuine kind, Castelli and Schueler remained in friendly contact. Castelli included Schueler's 'October' in his 1958 group show, which also included works by Jasper Johns and Robert Rauschenberg, and four others. Schueler at last

☐ 3

planned his return trip to New York, leaving Europe, a couple of months later, in January 1959. Castelli mounted another show of Schueler's French paintings in April 1959, and although a number of works sold, the show did not sell significantly well. Schueler, intuitive as ever, realised then that Castelli's interest could not be sustained. Later, another New York gallery gave him a show, including both Mallaig and Paris works, but only a single, small painting sold. Luckily, Schueler was able to teach at the Yale Summer School. Some time later, he made determined efforts to find a new gallery, but without success.

In 1959, he was commissioned by the Uris Buildings Corporation in New York to carry out a 64 by 12 foot mural to go in the Colgate-Palmolive building at 300 Park Avenue, an extremely unusual event at that time. Murals were not much in vogue and the best architects, such as Frank Lloyd Wright and Mies van der Rohe, felt that their buildings were themselves works of art. Unfortunately, despite a superb presentation of substantial working studies, the corporate decision was negative. The studies 'Time Has Three Suns' (1959) were shown by ACA Galleries this year. They related to Schueler's experiences of nature and sky. In an interview with Magda Salvesen, BH Friedman recalled:

> The 'Time Has Three Suns' studies come directly after Jon's return from France where his paintings contained a luminosity and a glow of radiant light not found previously. The studies were very closely related, although I'm sure Jon saw huge differences among them. There's this exciting flow of energy – you start with one thing, then move on and make changes, perhaps like variations on a theme in jazz. They are all good – museum quality, as they say. Other very beautiful paintings from 1959 and 1960 are related to the sun imagery of the six studies – although none has the same long, horizontal format or deals with the passage of the sun during three periods of the day within the same painting.[3]

On a later journey back in Scotland in June 1970, Schueler had a fearful and life-changing experience on the Sound of Sleat (when normally there would have been long days and light nights). The intensity of this experience forced him in terms of his complete identity to confront and recognise the extent to which death had played a central role in his life. He referred to the psychologically searing and destructive capacity of the sky on that June night and decided that his work 'must be a search and a requiem'. That was partly for his lost mother, who died when Schueler was only six months old; the maternal deprivation and absence haunted him all his life.

> The vision was intensely real, yet it was the most powerful abstraction – nature a cold, stately presence, remote and unconcerned, beyond man's definitions, his identifications, his attempts at understanding, oblivious to his emotion. Man could only be irrelevant in the face of this implacable event, this dark and light of eternal death. Everything about the Sound of Sleat that I might have remembered, every colour, shape or form, the identity of sky, land or water was destroyed and replaced by those events that I can only call the unearthly light, the dark, dark, rich beyond the black, the mass of grey, and the deep shimmering of a streak below, a presence more powerful, more beautiful, more seductive, more real than man's fantasies of poetry or joy or the damnation of his days.[4]

The sense of loss in infancy was made all the worse for him through his wartime experience as the navigating officer of a B-17 bomber. Here, he was incarcerated, in a womb-like navigator's compartment below the pilot's, and while he himself survived, he witnessed through the observation panel friends dying in the fullness of youth, parachutes not opening, others were burnt to oblivion.

Schueler was destined to live on for many years, with a new and fulfilling companion, Magda Salvesen, art historian and author, who joined him in 1971. But ever since that experience at Mallaig, on a black June night, his date with death was inscribed, and seemingly never far off. With Magda, he managed to harness the sense of loss, and

□ 4

□ 5

survive all vicissitudes for two productive and climacteric decades.

Such a remarkable career as Jon Schueler achieved is also profoundly middle-American in its resilience and in his independent-mindedness. Born himself in Milwaukee in the shadow of World War I he lived a painter's life to the full. We can understand later how he chose to be away from the hubris of New York in a wintry Scotland, which some might have thought almost masochistic, but at least to be tempting fate, just at the time when Leo Castelli was helping him to the pinnacle of New York School success to all the Manhattan dreams of an artist.

After the difficult 1960s, Schueler's career was somewhat redeemed in 1975 by the one-man show he was given at the Whitney. By 1970, and for the last two decades of his life, his paintings had evolved again, showing a more resolved, less tempestuous awareness of natural elements. The Whitney show revealed the beginnings of this tendency. Schueler had returned to the wellspring of his total inspiration, the skies of Mallaig, now at last together with Magda, his muse and companion. He painted a whole series of masterworks: these sprang, perhaps, from his Expressionist antecedents, but contained so much more poetic and elemental meaning, drawn from the experience of life and death, imbued still with memories of wartime conflict, but now resolved. JH Baur's appraisal of Schueler's work is probably the most succinct:

Jon Schueler has walked a difficult path between opposites. His paintings look

6

abstract but are not. The character of the Scottish coast, where he lives, speaks through these poetic canvasses with remarkable clarity and exactness. One has only to compare them with the Highland skies to understand how true the paintings are to the light, the atmosphere and the dramatic spirit of the place. And yet these are basically abstract pictures, not unrelated to the work of Mark Rothko or some of Clyfford Still's big canvasses. They have that kind of largeness, mystery and power. They strike a more precarious balance between observation and abstract form than do most paintings that try to wed the two – such as those of Milton Avery or Georgia O'Keeffe, to name at random artists who have succeeded in their own way. Schueler's solution is more difficult because it is less obvious. He risks more by deliberately exploring a narrow area where nothing is secure, where everything is changing, evanescent, and evocative. We see his paintings one minute as clouds and sea and islands, the next as swirling arrangements of pure colour and light.[5]

Accordingly, these New York and Edinburgh exhibitions in 2006 remind us now of the continuing and growing importance of Schueler; of his remarkable commitment and development as a mature painter, abstract, yet inspired by natural phenomena. Late works are often a major disappointment, but in Schueler's case, they represent a hard-won personal vindication. The new awareness comes when this planet, these astral phenomena, are subject to a new phase of global observation and concern. The sublime is with us, as never before, and in many guises. Since the historical marker of Schueler's outstanding talent, the 1975 Whitney show, there has not been any major Schueler exhibition. Institutionally, the time is now ripe for such an important retrospective.

JMcK

References
1. Nordland G, Ingleby R. *Jon Schueler, To the North*. London: Merrell, 2002: 32.
2. Banks R. Introduction. In: Salvesen M, Cousineau D (eds). *Jon Schueler, Sound of Sleat: A Painter's Life*. New York: Picador, 1999: 62–63.
3. Jon Schueler (1916–1992), *Time Has Three Suns*. New York: ACA Galleries, 2006: 6.
4. Norland G, Ingleby R. *Op cit*: 88.
5. *Ibid*: 35–36.

□ 1

Rediscovering the silver age of Russian art

Mir Iskusstva: Russia's Age of Elegance

Princeton University Art Museum, New Jersey

25 February–11 June 2006

While the recent, ambitious 'RUSSIA!' show at the Guggenheim Museum in New York was a bit thin on the artists associated with the Ballets Russes, the travelling exhibition, 'Mir Iskusstva: Russia's Age of Elegance', provides a compelling introduction to the twilight of the Tsars. The State Russian Museum in St Petersburg, in conjunction with the International Foundation for Arts and Education in Bethesda, MD, have pulled together more than 80 paintings, drawings, prints, sculpture, ceramics, posters, book and stage designs from the Silver Age of Russian Art. 'Mir Iskusstva' has already been shown at the Joslyn Art Museum in Omaha, NE and at the Weisman Art Museum in Minneapolis, MN, and finishes at the Princeton University Art Museum in New Jersey on 11 June.

'Mir iskusstva' means 'World of Art' and refers to an art magazine, a series of exhibitions and the artistic circle of Serge Diaghilev and Alexandre Benois. With their motto, 'Art for art's sake', many of the movement's designers may seem frivolous when compared with the intense, socially committed Modernists who succeeded them. The Soviet avant-garde came up with the term miriskusniki to describe all that was decadent and passé in contemporary art. The eclectic World of Art aesthetic might be called Russian Art Nouveau, in which style was more important than content. Benois and his associates embraced all the arts; the decorative as well as the plastic. The most famous manifestation of Mir iskusstva was the Ballets Russes, which brilliantly combined music, painting and dance. Diaghilev's productions (that were never actually performed in Russia) were famous for their bold colour and rampant sensuality, especially those designed by Leon Bakst; but there are surprisingly few costume and set designs in the current exhibit. The curators have concentrated on other areas of this movement that are less known in the West.

The most impressive works in the show are the portraits of many of Russia's literary, art and stage luminaries. Boris Kustodiev, the greatest of these portraitists, brought all the major figures of Mir iskusstva together in a handsome sketch of aesthetic unity and friendship for a group portrait that was never painted. Working in a manner reminiscent of

☐ 1. Boris Grigoriev. *Portrait of Vsyevolod Meyerhold,* 1916. Oil on canvas 247 x 163 cm.
Image courtesy of the State Russian Museum, St Petersburg

☐ 2

Whistler, Kustodiev captured the young charmer, Ivan Yakovlevich Bilibin, decked all in black and white except for a carmine carnation. Kustodiev redeems his rather tame self-portrait of 1905 with a monumental picture of the famous opera singer Fyodor Chaliapin at a winter fair. It is all the more remarkable when one learns that the artist was half-paralysed at the time he painted it. The same arrogant intelligence of Chaliapin is evident in Bakst's painting of Diaghilev, where the shock of premature white in his black hair lends the impresario the haughtiness of a pre-revolutionary male Susan Sontag. The creamy brush strokes of Konstantin Somov's picture of

his lover, Methodius Lukyanov, indicate exactly what attracted the painter to the elegant gentleman. Somov's portrait of the pianist Serge Rachmaninoff is far more conventional, having been commissioned in 1925 by the Steinway & Sons piano company to hang in the hall of their New York showroom.

Modernity creeps gently into some of these pictures. Cubist elements are evident in Yuri Grigoriev's portrait of the great director Vsevolod Meyerhold and Yuri Annenkov's portrait of the photographer Miron Sherling. These paintings perhaps belong more to the post-revolutionary Soviet Union than to the Silver Age. Less successful is cartoonist Nikolai

☐ 3

☐ 4

☐ 2. Igor Grabar. *Flowers and Fruit on a Piano,* 1904. Oil on canvas 79 x 101 cm. Image courtesy of the State Russian Museum, St Petersburg

☐ 3. Leon Bakst. *Supper,* 1902. Oil on canvas, 150 x 100 cm. Received in 1920 from the Alexander Korovin collection, Petrograd. Image courtesy of the State Russian Museum, St Petersburg

☐ 4. Andrei Ryabushkin. *They Are Coming (Muscovites Awaiting Entry of a Foreign Consul to Moscow in the late 17th Century),* 1901. Oil on canvas 204 x 102 cm. Image courtesy of the State Russian Museum, St Petersburg

☐ 5

☐ 6

Radlov's painting of the Symbolist poet Mikhail Kuzmin. It looks like a caricature. The most striking of these post-Cubist portraits is Natan Altman's 1915 picture of Anna Akhmatova. In her blue dress and bright yellow shawl, the angular poet looks like an elegant Slavic Virginia Woolf.

The women's portraits are more revelatory than the men's. The feline expression on the lady's face and the thrust of her supple body in Bakst's portrait of Benois' wife, 'Supper' (1902), oozes with the sexual allure the painter brought to his stage designs. The landscape artist, Anna Ostroumova-Lebedeva, never thought Valentin Serov's melancholy portrait of her captured her true spirit, but it is a stunning picture nonetheless. Russian painters are not famous for their nudes, and that may be why Serov's picture of the Jewish dancer, Ida Rubenstein, wearing nothing but rings on her fingers and toes, was as shocking to St Petersburg society in 1910 as Manet's 'Olympia' was to Parisians in 1865. While her brashness is still jarring, the picture is more a coloured drawing than a painting. The bisexual Rubenstein, who danced naked in a private performance of 'Salome', was in her day considered a great beauty; but today her charms have evidently faded. One of the pleasant discoveries of this show is the young Zinaida Serebryakova. Her pretty self-portrait of 1911 indicates that she herself must have posed over and over for the zaftig bathers in her shimmering 'Bath House' (1913). Her style might be called Russian Mannerism. It has all the polish, sheen and precision of the better known and vastly overrated Art Deco portraits of Tamara de Lempicka. The frank sensuality of Serebryakova's bathers is missing from Kuzma Petrov-Vodkin's oddly baleful orange nudes, like Cain and Abel on an emerald green hill beneath a cobalt blue sky.

Landscapes are few and far between at the Princeton University Art Museum, although there is a fine vigorous study of a provincial fair booth in winter by Kustodiev. Benois' views of Versailles are no more than lovely sketches. Ostroumova-Lebedeva's cool, elegantly balanced colour woodcuts of pre-revolutionary gardens, parks and palaces contrast beautifully with Mstislav Dobuzhinsky's rugged, frenetically charged lithographs of St Petersburg under reconstruction. The World of Art group became internationally known for their graphic works - everything from postcards to sheet music covers. Many Mir iskusstva artists were masters of book illustration and there is a fine smattering of children's book art by Benois, Bilibin, Dobuzhinsky, Dmitry Mitrokhin, Georgy Narbut and Elena Polenova. The Cotsen Children's Library within the Princeton University Library has mounted a small auxilliary exhibition, 'Mir Isskustva: Masterpieces of the Russian Picture Book', with the loveliest examples of the period. It is a shame the librarians leave the lights off in the cases.

Perhaps some restraint prevented the curators from including any of the more scandalous and sometimes scatological designs from Somov's notorious Beardsley-esque Le Livre de la Marquise (1918), perhaps the most infamous example of Russian erotica. The two drawings exhibited here are surprisingly chaste when compared to the lithe depravity of others in the volume. Somov's use of elegant visual double entendre in his ornate neo-Rococo silhouettes anticipated the more violent and politically charged work of the contemporary African American artist Kara Walker. Grigoriev and Mitrokhin, too, produced 'indecent' books missing from the Princeton exhibition.

The World of Art did not last long. Most members who survived the Revolution swiftly scattered to other parts of the globe. Even if 'Mir Iskusstva: Russia's Age of Elegance' does not fully explore all aspects of this doomed movement in Russian art, the show nevertheless includes many remarkable and rarely seen works by some of its most gifted and influential artists. **MPH**

☐ 7

□ 1

□ 1. Bernard Khoury. *BO18 Music Club*. Built 1998

Out of Beirut

Modern Art Oxford

13 May–16 July 2006

The work of 18 Lebanese artists has been brought together for this exhibition at Modern Art Oxford, many of them showing for the first time in the UK. Over 15 years may have passed since the end of Lebanon's civil war, but politics and memory are still major preoccupations for these artists: unsurprising in a country where the Prime Minister was assassinated last year by a car bomb, and whose civilian population is, at the time of writing, suffering in the resurgent conflict between Hezbollah and the Israeli Army.

The architect, Tony Chakar, whose work also appears in the show, asks in an email exchange recorded in the exhibition catalogue, 'Why is it that we cannot start talking about art – strategies, practices, or whatever – without first immersing ourselves in politics?'[1] This question, and its rhetorical assumption that, especially in Lebanon, art is not separable from politics, haunts the practices of these artists and gives rise to some powerful work.

The average visitor probably won't know the specific details of Beirut's past conflicts – in which case, Lamia Joreige's hour-long documentary film, 'Here and Perhaps Elsewhere', would make a good place to start. In what was, for me, the exhibition's most nuanced exploration of the interrelationship between memory and trauma, the artist walked the old 'green line' that divided Beirut into east and west, filming with a hand-held camera and asking the people she met the simple question, 'Do you know someone who was kidnapped here during the war?'

The documentary consists of their responses and recollections, and what soon emerges from the continual layering of testimony as she crosses neighbourhood religious boundaries is a sense of the precariousness of even recent history, and the realisation that all memories are to some extent unreliable. It is through inclusion and multiplicity, and the gradual accretion of details and stories - sworn to be true, or frankly acknowledged to be rumours - that the watcher of the film comes to understand something of the complexity of Beirut's traumatic history.

The majority of those kidnapped or 'disappeared' were civilians, taken by one or other of the militias in tit-for-tat responses as they tried to cross the lines, and often never seen again. At each crossing point, the picture freezes and fades into documentary photos of how the area looked in the war; the once-devastated landscape now vanished under new highways or buildings. The sound of building work and drilling carries through the streets in many of the mini-interviews, a counterpoint to the memories triggered by Joreige's questions. The film makes no claims to be part of some kind of healing process; on the contrary, it includes citizens who talk about the futility of remembering, one man exclaiming, 'How can I recount their names?' Another chides the artist, saying that by asking people to remember those who have vanished, without confirmation of death, she is cruelly reawakening the hope that they may still be alive.

Joreige's presence is elided into the shaky movements of the camera and the occasional prompting question, giving her subjects a certain autonomy. They use this freedom to take her questions in different directions: some recount neighbourhood gossip; others have forgotten entirely, or want to remember instead their relatives who were killed. Their other concerns intrude into the discussion: Iraq, Palestine and the economy. Joreige always asks for the disappeared's name: it is always given, a bald fact sitting astride blurred memories. In the last few minutes of the film, which is worth watching in its entirety, the artist asks another shopkeeper the by-now familiar question. One of the names reeled off catches her ear, and she asks more about this man, and the circumstances of his death. It turns out that he was her uncle.

In her catalogue essay, Kaelen Wilson-Goldie quotes one of Joreige's interviewees, who tells her there is no point in recording these stories 'because they won't give you the answer you're looking for'.[2] This is indeed the case if the artist is looking for some sort of historical truth; but it would appear that Joreige's project has less to do with this than with trying to understand how people have recovered or let slip their personal and collective memories of those who vanished. A related point Wilson-Goldie makes is that the civil war is in danger of becoming 'one overarching trauma which effectively masks over or represses many others',[3] such as token democracy or a non-independent judiciary; this is a risk that Joreige's film takes.

In the built environment, no less than in an individual's memory, versions of the past compete to influence the future. In an article in issue 99 of *Frieze* magazine, Tony Chakar summarised the planned reconstruction of Martyr's Square as an example of debate between two such conflicting visions:

Should Martyr's Square be open to the sea, thus becoming a Parisian-style boulevard, or should it remain an enclosed square, in the traditional style of medieval Arab cities? What was debated was obviously more than the mere morphology of a square [...] Latent in the debate was Lebanon's future.[4]

Bernard Khoury has attempted to duck such a discourse in designing BO18, a nightclub sited in The Quarantine, an area deeply scarred by a militia attack in 1976. The club is underground, depressed in order to 'avoid the over-exposure of a mass that could act as a rhetorical monument',[5] as Khoury puts it. His video piece for the exhibition is a night-time exploration of the club. At first, the site seems to be an almost derelict open space, filled with cars. The club is nearly invisible, a hole in the ground open to the sky. The camera peers down: lights, music and people dancing.

□ 2

□ 3

□ 4

Lebbeus Woods has made the case for 'new spaces of habitation constructed on the existential remnants of war', claiming that they 'do not celebrate the destruction of an established order, nor do they symbolise or commemorate it'.[6] Instead, he sees the physical scars of war as 'the beginnings of new ways of thinking, living and shaping space, arising from individuality and invention', and thus as an opportunity for a new type of community 'that precludes the hierarchical basis for organised violence and war'.[7]

The majority of post-war reconstruction in Beirut was entrusted to one building company, Solidere, owned by the future Prime Minister and assassination victim, Rafiq Hariri. Following the bombing that ended his life, mass demonstrations took place in Martyr's Square, with the protestors calling for, among other things, an end to the presence of Syrian troops in the country. Two of the works in the exhibition mark this event: Gilbert Hage's simple photos show ordinary citizens at the demos standing in front of a section of graffiti-covered wall, young and old alike, while Ziad Abillama's lo-fi video directs confrontational questions about Lebanon's future towards members of the public and records their responses. It's a pity that only a few of Hage's

photos are displayed in the gallery (160 are shown in the catalogue), as the value of the work surely lies in the cumulative effect of seeing recorded many of the individuals who came together in a (non-sectarian) protest.

Other works in the exhibition are compelling but more frustrating. Walid Raad's photographic plates 'We Can Make Rain But No One Came To Ask' are part of an ongoing project that is constructed around records of one particular explosion that took place in Beirut in January 1986. The plates are large, and mostly blank, with a thin strip running along the bottom like the line demarking the footnotes on an academic text. Looking closely, the line consists of photographic montages, with black and white portraits, location shots, news stills and reproductions of signatures and diagrams colliding. Beneath the line are sparse numbered footnotes in English, with the text cut in half horizontally to render it semi-comprehensible. The information seems to be hiding in the margins, trying to disappear (or being made to disappear) into the extra-lexical template of an authorised document. I was reminded in some ways of Xu Bing's A Book from the Sky, for which the Chinese artist diligently invented a totally meaningless language of some 4,000 characters, carved printing blocks for each one and produced a whole encyclopaedia of books, bound and formatted in the traditional Chinese manner, and scrolls many hundreds of non-words long. Both projects seem to share a distrust of words and the transmission of information, while paying homage to the ritual forms which information takes.

A fiction created by Joana Hadjithomas and Khalil Joreige, 'Wonder Beirut: the story of a pyromaniac photographer', demonstrates similar misgivings about published information. 'Abdallah Farah' is a postcard photographer whom the artists supposedly met in the 90s, who had published a series of photographs of Beirut's tourist attractions in the late 60s. As the civil war continued through the late 70s, 'Farah' started burning and damaging, little by little, the negatives that had produced the postcards, mirroring and then outdoing the destruction around him. The artists have 'reissued' these burnt images as a new set of postcards, full of tears, bubbles and lacunae. The visitor is encouraged to take these postcards away: they might function as a reminder of just what lies behind the recent reconstructions, or perhaps constitute a perverse act of triumph over adversity.

'Debate begins with the acquisition of culture', claims one of the interviewees in Abillama's film. But the two surely go hand in hand: culture, when it is growing and not ossifying, is the feeling-out of new spaces and new methods, a process for which debate is necessary. And, rightly enough, certain types of culture (of plurality, of non-certainty) foster debate. 'Out of Beirut' provides a snapshot of positive debates and cultural explorations taking place in the city; let us hope that, in spite of the physical and social damage Lebanon is facing, they continue to prosper. **JW**

References
1. Wright S. Territories of Difference: Excerpts from an E-mail Exchange between Tony Chakar, Bilal Khbeiz and Walid Sadek. In: Cotter S (ed). *Out of Beirut*. Oxford: Modern Art Oxford, 2006: 64.
2. Wilson-Goldie K. Contemporary Art Practices in Post-war Lebanon: An Introduction. In: *ibid:* 82
3. *Ibid:* 88.
4. Chakar T, Zolghadr T. 'City Report: Beirut'. *Frieze* magazine, May 2006.
5. Khoury B. BO18. In: *ibid:* 97.
6. Woods L. *War and Architecture, Pamphlet Architecture:* 15. New York: Princeton Architectural Press, 1993: 14.
7. *Ibid:* 19.

1

On Photography: A Tribute to Susan Sontag

Metropolitan Museum of Art, New York

6 June–4 September 2006

Susan Sontag's passionate engagement with photography is the subject of a small but intriguing bit of curatorial ingenuity; a show that offers a handful of Sontag's potent statements on the medium illustrated with images that provide point and counterpoint to her ideas. On view at New York's Metropolitan Museum of Art until 4 September 2006, the exhibit links two of Sontag's published volumes – *On Photography* (1979) and *Regarding the Pain of Others* (2004) – with approximately 40 photographs from the museum's collection, including two portraits of Sontag, one by Peter Hujar from 1975 and one in Petra, Jordan, by Annie Leibovitz from 1994. While Sontag's words are powerful and can alter the way visitors look at photographs for the rest of their lives, what emerges most strongly from the show is a clearer picture of Sontag herself.

A determined, outspoken woman, Sontag (1933–2004) first made an impact on the New York intellectual scene in the 1960s. She represented a new breed of New York intellectual. At first enamoured of the New York intellectual elite, eventually she alienated many of its members by championing a more democratic forum in which to discuss art and

literature, including subjects the others did not consider worthy of commentary.

Born in New York, Sontag was raised in Tucson, Arizona and Los Angeles, California. Her undergraduate years were spent at the College of the University of Chicago; later, she did graduate work in philosophy, literature and theology at Harvard and Saint Anne's College, Oxford. Her first published work was a novel (*The Benefactor,* 1963), and she has said that she considered herself a novelist. But soon after the book appeared she turned her attention to filmmaking and social activism. These activities and her curious, adventurous spirit took her around the globe. The four films she wrote and directed were made abroad: 'Duet for Cannibals' (1969) and 'Brother Carl' (1971) in Sweden; 'Promised Lands' (1974) in Israel during the October War (1973); and 'Unguided Tour' (1983) in Italy.

The wide range of her interests and intellect led to an interdisciplinary approach that excluded nothing and allowed for a variety of interpretations. Critics would question her boldness in taking on subjects in which she had little background, as well as the contradictions they detected in her views. What might seem contradictory was, perhaps, an expansion of

2

ideas in new dimensions. By nature, Sontag lived with her passions, turning them over in her mind until she could see every side and consider every angle. This is certainly true for her lifelong attraction to photographs; readers will notice a difference in tone and focus in On Photography, which collects essays that first appeared in the New York Review of Books, and Regarding the Pain of Others, which examines the morality and ethics of photography as a chronicle and instrument of war. It was published after Sontag had struggled with cancer (she died of leukaemia in December 2004) and seen a great deal of political and social strife at home and abroad.

War – or more precisely, images of war – haunted Sontag's imagination. As a youth, she claimed, a photo taken at a concentration camp changed her and made her very unsure of the world she had come to know. While the still-strong sense of justice available to children makes many of them highly sensitive to such images, as adults, photos of war tend to desensitise viewers, bringing them, as Sontag has pointed out, both closer to, and further from, reality. Sontag's sensitivity and idealism remained throughout her life. As an adult, she became involved in anti-war activism, traveling to Hanoi in 1968 after the US bombing and writing about her experiences (Trip to Hanoi). More recently, in summer 1993, she staged Samuel Beckett's Waiting for Godot in war-torn Sarajevo.

The mix of photographs in the exhibit mirrors the different dimensions and layers of meaning that photographs have in individual lives. On

the surface, they serve as an account of the truth; a reproduction of people and things seen in place and time. The semblance of veracity, Sontag maintained, was at the root of our obsession with photographs. By viewing these images, she said, people believe they can appropriate them, somehow access another person's experience, capture a memory for eternity or own an object. But the medium of photography, in fact, changes how we view what we normally see before our eyes. In 'Plato's Cave', from On Photography, she explained that photographs offer a 'new visual code' and create a new 'grammar and ethics of seeing'.

Some of the quotations come from essays in which Sontag discussed the actual work on view and/or the artist. A work by EJ Bellocq is accompanied by an excerpt from her introduction to Bellocq: Photographs from Storyville, the Red-Light District of New Orleans. Here she suggested the reason for Bellocq's popular appeal: 'the low-life material; the near mythic provenance (Storyville); the informal, anti-art look, which accords with the virtual anonymity of the photographer and the real anonymity of his sitters; their status as objets trouves and a gift from the past'.[1]

Other images are used to provide viewers with a chance to examine Sontag's words in context. An interesting juxtaposition is to consider the two portraits of Sontag in light of her words. In her introduction to Hujar's Portraits in Life and Death, she wrote that, 'Photographs instigate, confirm, seal legends. Seen through photographs, people become icons of themselves'. Hujar's striking portrait of

☐ 3. Robert Frank. *Fourth of July, Coney Island*, 1955.
Gelatin silver print. 10 x 14 in. (26 x 35.6 cm).
The Metropolitan Museum of Art.
Purchase, Alfred Stieglitz Society Gifts, 2002

Sontag exemplifies her words; here, Sontag reclines, her body in repose but her face set in an attitude of thought or contemplation. Perhaps Hujar had tried to grasp the quality of her active mind and her graceful, confident way of being in the world.[2]

Nearly two decades later, Leibovitz caught Sontag in a different pose, surrounded by age-old rock and an equally massive stone structure in Petra. The often-controversial figure whose physical presence drew attention here seems fragile. The work recalls words Sontag wrote in 1973 suggesting that photographs are 'memento mori' and that the process of photography allows the taker to access the subject's 'mortality, vulnerability, mutability'.[3]

Whether they reveal the daily stories of individual lives, serve as icons of a way of life or document world events, images, Sontag believed, always require viewers to add to the story. In Stephen Shore's 'American Surfaces', the artist created a pastiche of Middle America: the facade of a main street JC Penney Co; a household pet; a diner table not yet cleared of a meal. The images beg viewers to fill in the details, to remember times from their own past and participate in an era now gone.[4] The intimacy of these photographs comes just before an image by Walker Evans in which Evans affirmed a way of life he considered noble, one with inherent value and stability. Shore's scenes are the ephemeral currency of the daily – idiosyncratic moments attached to specific people and places – and sharply contrast with Evans' work, where the persona of the taker is masked by the subject.

Among the other artists included in the show are Robert Frank, Edward Steichen, Andy Warhol, Robert Mapplethorpe and Berenice Abbott. The variety of selections - portraits, surreal still-lifes, dramas of public and private life – offer visitors many opportunities to test Sontag's statements and explore their own attraction to photographs. A crusader for the issues and things she cared deeply about, Sontag left us words and ideas filled with passion. In the end, *On Photography* is a celebration of Sontag's vision and passionate life. **CDM**

References
1. Szarkowski J. *Bellocq: Photographs from Storyville, the Red-Light District of New Orleans*. London: Random House, 1996.
2. Hujar P. *Portraits in Life and Death*. New York: Da Capo Press, 1977.
3. Sontag S. *On Photography*. London: Penguin Books, 1979.
4. Shore S. *American Surfaces*. New York: Phaidon Press, 2005.

3

Peter Zumthor: Summerworks

Royal Academy of Arts Summer Lecture, London

3 July 2006

The Royal Academy lecture, 'Peter Zumthor: Summerworks', was given by the Swiss architect Peter Zumthor to a packed audience. The event was heavily oversubscribed. It was a brilliant tour de force, delivered in a somewhat conversational, deadpan manner. The architect seemed more like an Alpine farmer, modest yet canny. If one came across Zumthor on a mountain pass, appropriately near to his home (perhaps amid the sound of goat bells and the soft resonance of mountain streams) he would seem to be the kind of natural being who could stop and pass the time of day, as he did on this occasion at the Royal Academy.

But such ruminations would not be over-extended, and a touch of self-protective steel would be detectable. For how else could Zumthor have scaled the heights of the architectural world, where he stands today, slightly bemused, but certain of how it is? Certainly, as he has done to countless students, he would ensure that no one got lost in this arduous and treacherous terrain. He is essentially a guide across. Zumthor showed examples of his work in detailed context. Introduced into the narrative, quite deliberately to reassure, were images of his own studio/home, which emphasised the extent to which this realm is intertwined with that of his studio. These two domains become as one. The sequence of works shown ranged from a chapel

built at Metternich in Germany, to a light and elegant well-shaded lakeside restaurant on the island of Ufnau in Lake Zurich, both exemplifying the special collusion of rigour and serendipity. A city centre scheme (Tribschen 2006) for Lucerne revealed how Zumthor can design on any scale. The ingredient always present is a strand of recurrently poetic emphasis, which weaves together many previously discordant aspects. A building set into a steep gradient, for thermal baths, at Vals, Graubunden, exhibits a critical dialogue with the place occupied there, a process of carving into the mountainside. Likewise, the housing scheme settled into green woodland at Biel-Benken, Baselland, is where Zumthor distils the essence of the German/Swiss/Austrian 'siedlung' or housing settlement, where one side of the enclosure is open, allowing an interaction with the surrounding landscape.

In his much sought after small book (more like a book of poems) entitled *Thinking Architecture,* Zumthor has set out the way in which he looks at architecture: 'a way of looking at things'. In his search for the 'lost architecture', reminiscences here from a life of design and practice (where research inevitably and invariably leads) vie with his childhood memories. Door handles, flagstones, different ways of closing and opening doors and windows, give together 'the reservoirs of architectural images that I explore as an architect'. The assuming of poetic qualities comes only if 'the architect is able to generate a meaningful situation for these, since materials in themselves are not poetic', but the inherent, sensuous qualities redeem the previously insensate materials, 'making them shine and vibrate'. One is reminded of a recent definition by Susan Sontag, in her introduction to the re-publication of the long lost Russian author Leonid Tsypkin's 'Summer in Baden-Baden' where 'it is not docu-novel' and 'several real worlds are evoked, described, re-created in a hallucinatory rush of associations'. Tsypkin preferred the films of Antonioni to those of his compatriot Tarkovsky. In the real worlds evoked by Zumthor, there occur seams of memory, about materiality become poetry, such as the cooler essence of Antonioni as compared to the dramatic progressions of Tarkovsky. Unwittingly I guess ... for Zumthor, too, there is an echo of Peter and Alison Smithson's thinking, as expressed in their book *Ordinariness and Light* (1970), where they chart a materiality of buildings (as expressed in their own St Hilda's College, Oxford). But Zumthor's memory sources and references go much further, in looking at John Berger, Italo Calvino, Edward Hopper, Joseph Beuys, Arte Povera and Per Kirkeby. Where, asks Zumthor, is the hard core of beauty? The composer John Cage, and the philosopher Martin Heidegger in Building, Dwelling, Thinking provide some further admissible evidence for the architect.

Zumthor lives and works now in a farming village set in the mountains, Graubunden. He refers always to buildings that distil 'the essence of place'. At various stages in his book he seeks out this essence. Zumthor says, 'the relationship of man to places and through places to spaces is based on his dwelling in them'. In expounding, through his buildings, and the memories that they evoke, his sense of architecture, Zumthor provides a refreshing, perhaps brilliant insight into the fundamentals of creative perception. If society in its breathless contemporary pursuit of 'quality' forgets such simple meanings, the buildings of the future will remain predominantly arid or sensationalist. Perhaps Zumthor could be said to have brought architects to their senses before it is too late.

The Royal Academy is to be congratulated for inviting Peter Zumthor to deliver this annual exhortation. As Zumthor said: *'The very core of my work is staying at home, forgetting the world around me and submerging myself completely in the tasks I have to do, the places I have to work for, the atmospheres I want to create. Research, the joy of working, of finding a form for an everyday ritual, for a special moment in the future life of a building not yet known; the pleasures of working together with my collaborators, young architects, in a concentrated way, in a specific environment where there is the light of the sun entering from the garden of flowers and maples, and food and drinks, and every once in a while my grandson, visiting me from across the street, Summerworks. Splendid concentration. My lecture will report on the outcome of that'.*

Peter Zumthor. *Thinking Architecture*. Birkhauser (second and expanded edition, 1996)

The Eames Lounge Chair:
An Icon of Modern Design

Museum of Arts and Design, New York

18 May–3 September 2006

Grand Rapids Art Museum, Grand Rapids, Michigan

6 October–31 December 2006

Henry Ford Museum, Dearborn, Michigan

3 February–29 April 2007

The Eames Lounge Chair: An Icon of Modern Design, by Martin Eidelberg,

Thomas Hine, Pat Kirkham, David Hanks and C Ford Peatross is published by Merrell,

price £29.95 in hardback (ISBN 1 85894 302 7)

The Eames Lounge Chair is very hard to categorise as a type. Possibly, it can be said to be part of a broader design idiom that emerged in American culture in the 1950s, including the Boeing Superfortress aircaft (or indeed the subsequent Boeing Stratocruiser airline), the US Army original jeep, the small truck, or the Lincoln Zephyr Coupe automobile (recent selling pitches by Lincoln for their 2006 Zephyr model astutely emphasise the Eames inspiration for the seats!) This idiom is unselfconsciously but mechanistically common to all: as informal products of an effortless self-confidence about a robust 'fitness for purpose' – running from the most basic specifications to an indisputable luxury – these designs, indeed, seem to us today both unselfconscious and non-prescriptive. But they are all, to a greater or lesser extent, design icons. How was this achieved?

The Eames Lounge Chair and its exhibition came to New York earlier this year, hosted by the Museum of Arts and Design. We learn in the catalogue of the discussions that took place between curators to plan the exhibitions in January 2004, which endeavoured to position

☐ 1. Charles and Ray Eames, Charles Kratka and staff, *Exploded drawing of Lounge Chair components,* with hand lettering by Sister Corita Kent of Immaculate Heart College, c. 1956. Courtesy Herman Miller, Inc. Source Eidelberg M *et al.* The Eames Lounge Chair: An Icon of Modern Design

☐ 2. 'Herman Miller presents an upholstered lounge chair designed by Charles Eames', Herman Miller advertising, c. 1956, Library of Congress, Manuscripts Division, The Work of Charles and Ray Eames. Source: Eidelberg M *et al.* The Eames Lounge Chair: An Icon of Modern Design

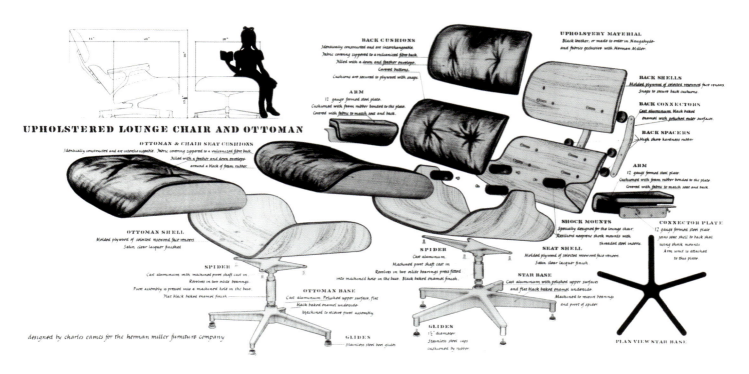

□ 1

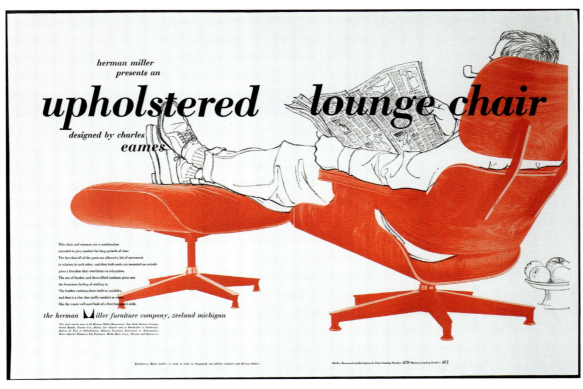

□ 2

3

☐ 3. Ray Eames, *Untitled,* 1943, plywood sculpture, Library of Congress, Prints and Photographs Division, The Work of Charles and Ray Eames. Source: Eidelberg M *et al*. The Eames Lounge Chair: An Icon of Modern Design

☐ 4. Ray Eames, *Sketch of Chairs,* c. 1943-46, graphite on tracing and kraft paper, Library of Congress, Prints and Photographs Division, The Work of Charles and Ray Eames. Source: Eidelberg M *et al*. The Eames Lounge Chair: An Icon of Modern Design

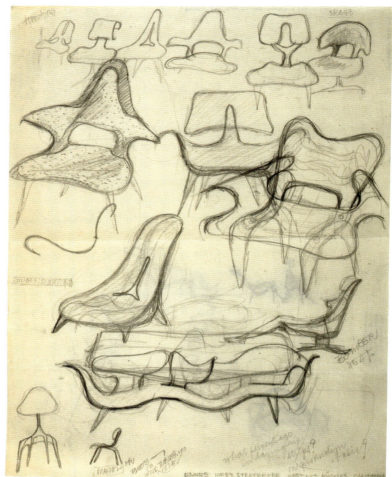

☐ 4

the Chair historically and culturally. 'What were the characteristics of its cultural moment in mid-1950s America? What did possession of such a chair say about its owners – that they were modern in personal style and open to ideas, comfortable in their skins?' The continuing and long-term commitment to design of Herman Miller, the producer, was a significant element. As the curators sat, well intentioned, in a wide circle of Eames Lounge Chairs, they wrestled with such definitions. It has to be said that, curiously, the Chair never seems to 'work' when grouped in such a way, whether paired in fours or sixes. It is a single icon, positioned in space, and not really subject to repetitive installation. But these wise discussions still bore fruit, as the swivels swivelled across the circle. 'Were they modern in personal style, open to ideas, comfortable in their skins? Did that describe us as we communally lounged?' asked the curators (as reported by Celeste Adams, Director at Grand Rapids).

In the catalogue there is a lengthy argument by one of these curators, Martin Eidelberg, Emeritus Professor of Art History at Rutgers University, entitled 'Charting the Iconic Chair'. This article comprehensively explores the view that the chair cannot be positioned in any European-derived trajectory of modern furniture. The full sequence of chairs is surveyed, from Josef Hoffmann in Vienna, to Marcel Breuer's Wassily Club Chair and the path pioneered in the 1930s by the Finnish master Alvar Aalto in the use of moulded plywood. Eidelberg explains in detail how

Aalto's 'breakthrough' in moulded plywood evolved, (as demonstrated in his famous 'Springleaf' armchair (1933). Laminated wood is employed for the frame, and plywood for the seat and back. Aalto's chairs were first exhibited in 1938 at the Museum of Modern Art in New York. The development of the Eames Lounge Chair came relatively late on the American scene, influenced partly by Aalto and Eero Saarinen. Conceived originally in 1953–54, it was not ready for production launching until 1956. Eidelberg affirms that in terms of innovation, the Eames Lounge Chair was not entirely far advanced. It had a reassuring 'comforting' idiom - not too modern at all: but that all worked. The fact that there were 50 steps, no less, in the assembly of the many parts (which denied some aspects of the prevailing Modernist ethos). It indicated, 'a shift away from the puritan asceticism of the first half of

□ 5

the 20th century. 'Was the Lounge Chair successful because of its unabashed combination of Modernity and traditionalism?' asks Eidelberg, perhaps playfully. Was it not a frontrunner for post-Modernism? Robert Venturi in his famous manifesto work, 'Complexity and Contradiction in Architecture' (Museum of Modern Art Papers on Architecture 1966; 1) certainly did not rise to the bait, nor did Charles Jencks in his later prognosis. Maybe the Eames Lounge Chair, in its very uniqueness, and all-American 1950s nature, was just too difficult to define.

The Eames Lounge Chair would seem to be prone to copying on account of its quality, but despite a bout of this in the 1990s, this has been legally prevented. The mere fact that there are so many stages in the actual assembly of the Chair seems to have acted anyway as a major deterrent. In a recent US court decision in favour of the Herman Miller Company that still produces it in Michigan, the key characteristics that now define the Eames Chair have been codified clearly as follows:

- Smooth, curved, moulded shells: the lounge chair having three shells, the ottoman having one
- The moulded shells being exposed from below

the ottoman and from the back, sides, and underside of the chair
- The edges of each moulded shell being exposed from the front of the lounge chair and ottoman
- Each of the moulded shells being shaped like a flattened 'u'
- Each moulded shell with cushioned upholstery
- Each moulded shell having 'buttons' that create permanent creases in the upholstery
- The back of the lounge chair consisting of two moulded shells, connected in the rear by two exposed bars, each bar being angled to tilt the upper moulded shell slightly forward of the lower moulded shell
- The angled bars spaced from the shells
- Upholstered armrests that extend downward into the chair and connect the two moulded back shells to the moulded seat shell.
  (See Herman Miller FED App. O337P)

The Eames Lounge Chair never seems to have furnished exotic suites in the movie world – yet it seems right for Raymond Chandler movie set pieces. It seems sadly to have been overlooked by Alfred Hitchcock for 'North by Northwest', where it would have been a perfect fit for the duplicitous spy played by James Mason. But taste always moves on, in the hands of its media arbiters. In a photo shoot from the early 1990s, the catalogue records how the fresh-faced Steve Jobs of Apple (bare-footed) and ever youthful Bill Gates of Microsoft sit posed in a relaxed mood: Jobs is in the chair, while Gates flatters him by squatting on the ottoman beside him. Here, the Eames Lounge Chair has moved to pole position as the seat of real and ultimate power, in this early 1991 colour shot of 'informal, but total control'. Each item of furniture projects a telling narrative (with hindsight from 15 years later) about the two owners. In his catalogue essay, Thomas Hine tries keenly to position this icon in terms of the collective culture and, ironically, only partly succeeds as he shows in the era of the failed 1950s Ford Edsel car – revealing the downside of the first post-war consumer surge. As Hine postulates, the Chair fitted the moment when, 'most Americans felt they could lead more luxurious lives'. But sales were never dramatic, even if steady: it took half a century to sell over 100,000 Chairs. The Edsel was a commercial failure, by contrast, but in the three years of actual production, the same number of cars were sold, such was the strength of the US economy at that time. And, of course, virtually all the Edsels have gone to a pressing engagement: the chair, by contrast, priced at $578 dollars with footstool in 1956, is still manifestly very much around. They last well, and today the resale value is about $4,500 altogether (2,756 were sold in 2004). What is not often realised is the extent to which the Eames' experience in designing a moulded

plywood leg splint for the US Navy (1943), itself a beautiful object, fed into the development of the Chair. This, of course, follows a production development sequence not uncommon where wartime products lead to useful peacetime spin-off. At the other end of the chronology there is a very revealing inclusion in the catalogue of the numerous advertising and promotional techniques used to market the chair. Self-evidently, too, this expanded the milieu of the Chair to include its users as Martin Scorsese, Saul Bellow, Arthur Miller and, in Britain, Tom Stoppard, all comfortable possessors of the icon. The Chair seems to have been a special predilection of intellectuals, rising academics and design-oriented executives. This single, pivotal resting place allows the occupant to survey all, and to presume to be master of all he (or she) surveys. It seems that more often than not 'she' is relegated to the slimmer Aluminium Group Lounge Chair and footstool, in all their elegance, likewise also free to pivot and pivot. Occasionally, the icon occupant would sport a pipe in earlier days, but no longer. In young families, the Chair becomes a permanently revolving roundabout. Which is where this writer himself came in, and his young children, circa 1970, all thanks to Zeev Aram, formerly of Kings Road, Chelsea. This particular Charles Eames Lounge Chair has survived two generations of dynamics. None were actually conceived in the Chair, but it's always possible. Long live this contemporary, global masterpiece: and 'salut' to both Charles and Ray Eames in this timely commemoration.

Editor

Pallant House

In August, this website featured an assessment of the high quality of the collections at Pallant House, Chichester. As promised in that article, here follows a more detailed appraisal of the new architecture of Pallant House itself.

This building is a remarkable achievement in design terms – a kind of symbolic recognition of the architects' achievement in the case of the British Library, and yet also a building all of its own, in the centre of an extremely high-quality cathedral city with all the environmental safeguards this would entail. Sir Colin St John Wilson and his partner (and wife) MJ Long, have applied the same design integrity that developed from 'The Other Tradition of Modernism' as Wilson calls it; a tradition that rejects the superficial definitions of so-called postmodern architecture, and argues for something more substantial. In this respect it is worth recognising here the high priority that the architects have placed on sustainable energy systems. Pallant House incorporates now a wholly contemporary geothermal heating and cooling system, which in order to reduce dependency on fossil fuels, harnesses the inherent natural resources, including the actual thermal capacity of the ground underneath the building. There being no available government subsidy for this kind of advanced technical solution, the full £80,000 funding for this highly original system had to be found from other sources.

Fortunately, calculations show that the new system is efficient enough to permit the installation's cost to be recouped within the foreseeable future. It is all the more surprising then that Pallant House is virtually unique in exploiting such a system (other than in an Oxford College). Eric Parry, reviewing the building for *Architecture Today* (July 2006), rightly claimed that Pallant House 'rests firmly in an English tradition of individual philanthropy born of addictive collecting set against the grain of institutional lethargy'. One might also add here that the Sackler Galleries at the Royal Academy of Arts, supported with such dedication by the late Dr Arthur Sackler and his widow (Dame) Jillian Sackler, inserted so skillfully by Lord Foster within two blocks of the existing building, also demonstrate this quality.

The new ground level is organised to offer freedom of movement in space: it is planned around a courtyard, which neatly nonetheless delineates the boundaries of new and old. The courtyard (designed by prize-winning garden architect Christopher Bradley-Hole) undoubtedly benefits from the planting of six semi-mature plane trees. Above the courtyard, a large window offers an axial view directly across to the arched stair window of the original Pallant House. This conversation between the original Pallant House and the new galleries seems to be entirely benign, each complimenting the other. At ground level again, one is aware of the spatial interaction of the inner courtyard with the entrance hall from the street: but this is an easy progress, without any degree of compulsion. The new galleries provide an extremely rich array of facilities, with a strong provision of prints and drawings gallery, library, workshop and seven

☐ 2

□ 2. *Courtyard image*. Photograph by Anne-Katrin Purkiss, 2006

□ 3. *Courtyard image*. Photograph by Peter Durant, 2006

varied galleries linking ultimately to Pallant House itself. The importance of such linkage cannot be stressed enough: in no way could the new just be bolted onto the old. The 20th-century collections of Dean Hussey and Wilson merge seamlessly together. Such is the ethos of the place that old and new harmonise readily together. The combination at ground level of ceiling lighting and peripheral indirect lighting from the courtyard mediates inside and outside. The first floor exhibition spaces maximise the potential of the available space. Here, the galleries are top lit by the use of an ingenious system of light wells. The key gallery is 21 m by 6.5 m wide, and straddles a long 45 m east-west 'spine', with six galleries opening off. Some ingenuity is deployed in creating multifunctional space here, to incorporate lecture-cum-seminar/workshop spaces. The conservatory, with its elegant window looking back over to the Pallant House stair window, creates, when required, a space for reading and study, and even casual browsing. The smell of coffee from below might eventually lure even the most dedicated user down to the restaurant or the garden tables, in what is a veritable suntrap.

□ 3

The exterior 'match' of the new galleries with old Pallant House is very subtly achieved by means of a recessed stair tower, handsome in terracotta cladding. The passer-by is not intimidated by 'boring old art' as runs the slogan of Pallant House today ('Its not for boring old art'). This might echo the sentiments of the average Chichester inhabitant: instead, a new world awaits, gently persuasive. The transition from the street frontage shared with the facade of Pallant House's grandiose merchant's town house, is somewhat uncompromising, and all the better for this. The other tradition of modernism is vindicated, whatever Betjeman and Pevsner might together find to argue with. For the first time since the Cathedral, in the new Pallant Galleries, Chichester has a mainstream example of European state-of-the-art architecture. **Editor**

Beyond the Palace Walls: Islamic Art from the State Hermitage Museum

Royal Museum of Scotland, Edinburgh

14 July–5 November 2006

'Beyond the Palace Walls: Islamic Art from the State Hermitage Museum' is a very timely collaboration for the Edinburgh Festival 2006 between the Royal Museum in Edinburgh and the State Hermitage Museum in St Petersburg. It follows, perhaps more boldly and confidently, the first mutual collaboration of the two museums at last year's Edinburgh Festival, entitled 'Nicholas and Alexandra: the Last Tsar and Tsarina'. This year, the State Hermitage Museum has made available the most select Islamic exhibits in their possession. Unlike the former exhibition, this offers a very much more topical focus on Russia's earlier relations with her neighbouring Islamic nations and peoples, with whom she has been deeply engaged over several centuries. In the Winter Palace at St Petersburg it was possible for the joint curators to draw together for this festival exhibition some 200 remarkable works of art. What is immediately revealed here is the boundless, timeless nature and quality of Islamic art, as it impinged across the borders of the Russian Empire from the heartlands and key centres of the Islamic world that lay to the south. What has been assembled is a unique array of ceramics, textiles, glass, arms and art.

Perhaps the most dramatic set piece displayed in the Royal Museum is a large, official tent, into which exhibition visitors can wander through a single opened side. This is a square structure, with a simple duo-pitched roof. Externally, it is impressive chiefly for its size, but this lack of decoration is in complete contrast to the interior, which combines highly decorated fabrics. While not quite in the realm of a conspicuous display of wealth, it conveys high importance of status on the part of its owner/occupant. The 19th-century English poet Samuel Taylor Coleridge wrote of Xanadu, with its 'stately pleasure dome'. This is probably in a different class of importance, but much of that opulent aesthetic is suggested by this construct. Internally, this tent of high officialdom (probably that of a general of high rank, used as a campaign tent), was carefully adopted without apparent damage by the Tsarist officers who took it in charge as captured booty. After use in

□ 2

□ 3

the rival army of the Tsar, it was finally sent to the Hermitage in 1848.

This Imperial tent thus forms the high point of the exhibition. Tents, it is explained in the catalogue, formed an important part of the process of progression of an army: in the Ottoman army, a corps of tent-pitchers existed to move a whole city of such tents to the next encampment en route. The tents themselves were of varying degrees of decorated opulence. The aesthetic of the interiors would combine an 18th-century eclectic style comprising elements from Islamic, East Asian and European cultures. The tent reveals here fabric window openings with hanging astragals, which let in light through gold ribbon lattices, revealing beautifully decorated, jewel-like and embroidered walls rising to a highly decorated internal roof lining, replete with landscape depictions of 'stately pleasure-domed' country manors in a tree-lined pasture. All this is in imitation of the actual aesthetic of the interior of Ottoman palaces. The silken wall panels carry joyful flower vase motifs. The actual latticework windows were made from pleated silk combined with gold and metal thread. By comparison, the exterior of the tent remains entirely simple with a plain light green exterior of a canvas-like fabric.

The diplomatic and commercial importance of developing long-maintained over-land trade routes between Russia and Islamic countries in some ways mirrors the sea-borne expansion of western European trade routes. Beyond, the full impact of Chinese Imperial culture is epitomised by an original ninth-century Tang vase on show: however, the subsequent skill of Islamic craftsmen to copy meticulously large ceramic pieces is revealed by a beautiful (but imitation) dish with a superb cobalt blue pigment, yet actually carrying the device of four-symbol Imperial China as a mark. Fortunately this didn't take in the St Petersburg Hermitage. Early 16th-century Ottoman armour and a helmet are displayed together to great effect. From a later period, a Qajar full-length female portrait vies with Ali Shah's elegant figure, holding a pose apparently adapted from the 1810 coronation portrait of Napoleon I (by Francis Gerard). From a much earlier epoch, by contrast, is displayed a beautiful gouache of 1602 from Iran of a girl in a fur hat by Riza-i Abbasi.

Weapon displays include a rifle decorated with coral (a flintlock piece). A 19th-century gold saddle stands nearby, as presented to Tsar Alexander I by the Khan of Khugan. The Russian priesthood were also seduced by such Islamic decorative skills. A late 17th-century cape, of Iranian silken velvet, reveals the influence of Turkish design, having also a motif of trees and flowers in serried rows. The main section of this exhibition focuses on the cultures of 'the Tulip and the Lotus', the golden age of Islamic art, between the 14th and 19th centuries, showing the continued interaction of East and West.

'Beyond the Palace Walls', as an exhibition, prompts some British celebration of the recent opening of the new Islamic art rooms at the Victoria and Albert Museum. The five centuries-old Ardabil carpet, originally commissioned for the Ardabil mosque in the north-west of Iran, was intended to embellish the shrine of Persia's original Shia rulers. Now, the new Jameel Gallery of Islamic Art there has placed the carpet on the floor, within its own non-reflecting glass container. This has allowed the superb colours to be fully evident, which would not have been so on a wall. The Ardabil comes

from a time when the Ottoman Sunnis had been displaced, and the Shias had instead consolidated their hold on Persia. The effect of such political contrasts has of course continued in the Islamic world.

There can, everywhere today, come a renewed respect for Islamic art, a development not reversed by the recent conflicts. In Europe and America, wide misconceptions exist about Moslem cultures and a process of redemption is long overdue in the museum world. The collaboration of the Hermitage and the Royal Museum in Edinburgh, and the Victoria and Albert Museum's new initiative, are both steps towards this process of cultural renewal. The Islamic world is not in denial and regression. It is alive today. In this connection there will continue to be reverses, too, like the departure of Donny George, the Curator of the Iraqi Museum from Baghdad, to Syria, who has found the working environment in the multicultural antiquities department there unsustainable.

Editor

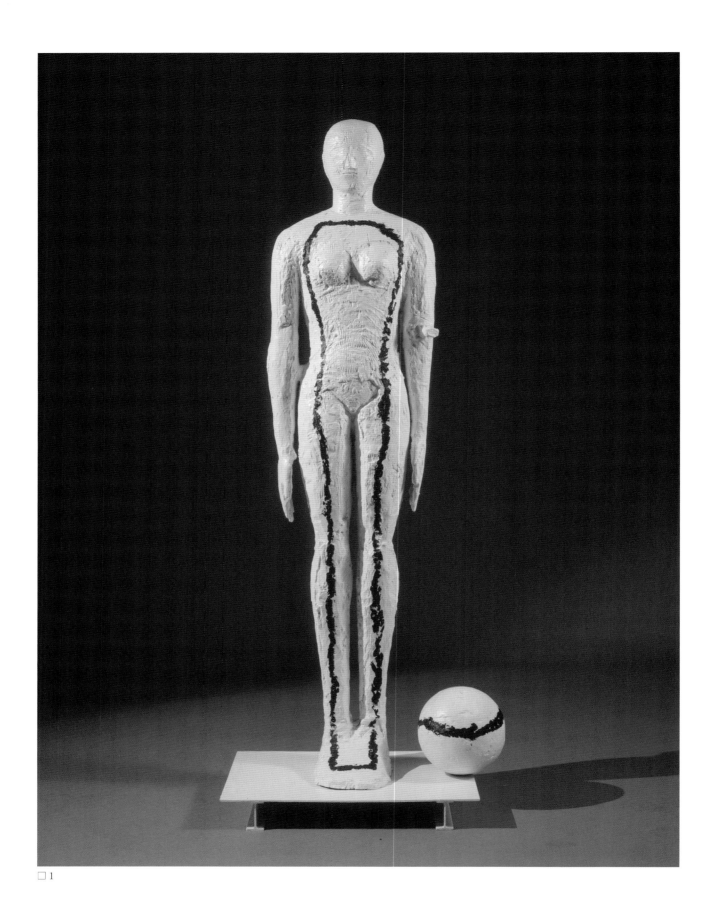

□ 1. Mimmo Paladino, *Untitled*, 2005. Painted aluminium (unique), 74 x 30 x 19 in/199 x 77 x 48 cm
© The artist, courtesy Waddington Galleries, London

Mimmo Paladino:
Black and White

Waddington Galleries, London, April-May 2006.

Royal Academy Summer Exhibition, London, 2006.

*I don't want to impose any point of view,
any perspective, because I'm also quite
fascinated by how others view my work. An
outsider's glance shows me what I don't
already know, what I haven't as yet seen. It's
a provocative experience.*[1]

In London, Mimmo Paladino's show, Black
and White, at the Waddington Galleries
earlier this year, and his spectacular large
painting, at the Royal Academy Summer
Exhibition, reveal his continued mastery of the
evocative and mysterious language of painting.
Paladino is working at the height of his powers,
on a grand scale, and to great effect. His work is
instantly recognisable, drawing on the deep
recesses of the memory and myth of Italy and
years of dedicated work as an artist. Paladino
uses numerous aspects cultural history,
especially Italian history. He works in painting,
printmaking and sculpture where drawing
underpins all of his work.

Born in Benevento in Southern Italy in 1948,
Mimmo Paladino grew up mostly in Naples. He
came into prominence with the artists known as
the 'Transavantguardia', a group defined by
Achille Bonita Oliva in 1979, which included
seven young Italian painters: Sandro Chia,
Francesco Clemente, Enzo Cucchi and Mimmo
Paladino, along with Nicola De Maria, Luigi

Ontani and Ernesto Tatafiori. 'Their subject-
matter, ranging from the classical to the
scatological, seemed unimaginably eclectic and
appeared to offer rich possibilities for a
continued life of art, which shortly before had
seemed to be talking itself into a self-reverential
corner'.[2]

Italian art in the 1970s, had been dominated
by the non-painters of Arte Povera. Arte Povera
chose installations of ready-mades, and found
materials; the artists rejected all evidence of the
artist's touch or signature, deemed as a form of
devalued subjectivity. Artists of the
transavantguardia, on the other hand, embraced
painting and emphasised the idiosyncratic. If
Arte Povera belonged to the avant-garde, the
transavantguardia was revivalist, choosing
painting, the medium which most epitomised
tradition in art. In Italy the choice was invariably
informed by the glorious history of Italian
painting from the medieval fresco painting to the
triumph of the Italian Renaissance. Achille
Bonita Oliva, who coined the term, organised the
first exhibition of the group in Sicily in 1979. He
published an article on the movement the same
year in Flash Art, and a book in 1980. The new
art movement quickly commanded an important
position in the international arena, dominating
the Venice Biennale of 1980. Oliva described the
transavantguardia, as being unlike the notion of

□2

modernist art which saw its development as
being from traditional to the new. The
transavantguardia opted, 'to pick and choose
from [past styles] in the conviction that, in a
society in transition toward an undefinable end,
the only option is that offered by a nomadic and
transitory mentality'.[3] Mimmo Paladino
described it as, 'crossing the various territories
of art, both in a geographical and temporal
sense, and with a maximum technical and
creative freedom. So if, on the one hand, I feel
close to Giotto and Piero della Francesca, on the
other I pay attention to Byzantine and Russian
icons...I believe that the superficial glance is very
much in keeping with the fast moving times we
live in'.[4]

Critics of the revival of painting, or perhaps
the particular form of its manifestation, in both
Italy and Germany in the 1980s, condemned the
new work as essentially retrograde, as quoting
the fascist styles of the 1930s, or glorifying

Italy's notoriously decadent Roman past. In
1981, the exhibition curated by Germano Celant
at the Pompidou Centre in 'Paris: Italian
Identity: Art in Italy since 1939', infuriated the
transavantguardia by all but excluding them.
Only one artist of the group was included (De
Maria). Celant continued to champion Arte
Povera, as well as minimalist performance and
conceptual art. As late as 1989 Celant had
accepted a number of artists (Cucchi, Clemente,
Kiefer) but still regarded the new painting as
nationalistic and apolitical and characterised
instead by a personal vision in the guise of
'beautiful painting' that would seduce the
viewer into believing it was a superior or 'real'
form of art. It was in Celant's view, nostalgic,
superficial and unacceptably showy. The
international/regional debate took place around
the world at this time. According to Oliva,
Italian artists had denied their national identity
for 35 years. With the transavantguardia, "The

☐ 3

idea of investigating the Italian-ness of Italian art, long discredited by its association with fascist cultural politics, was rehabilitated as the birthright of young painters.[5]

Irving Sandler identifies the dominant issues in the development of the movement in the 1980s.

Anticlassical classicism had long been a practice in Italian art; in the twentieth century, it was most commonly identified with de Chirico ... Like de Chirico the transavantguardia cleverly put references to 'Italianness' in figurative quotation marks. Nonetheless, the effect was peculiarly Italian. As Chia summed up, the special role of the artist was, 'to perceive what is given as a cultural tradition [in an] unconventional, outrageous way. It is his task and also his social duty ... to start a new creation from an existing creation'.[6]

Norman Rosenthal has chronicled the work of Mimmo Paladino and the artists of the

☐ 2. Mimmo Paladino, *Camera di Brancusi,* 2005. Oil on canvas, 94 1/2 x 133 7/8 in/240 x 340 cm © The artist, courtesy Waddington Galleries, London

☐ 3. Mimmo Paladino, *Esercizio di Lettura 4,* 2005–1998. Oil on canvas, 95 1/4 x 114 in/242 x 290 cm © The artist, courtesy Waddington Galleries, London

transavantguardia from the early 1980s. The
New Spirit in Painting was organised in 1981,
and the Italian Art in the 20th century: Painting
and Sculpture, 1900–1988, was organised by
him at the Royal Academy, London in 1989,
where he wrote the catalogue Introduction and
the essay on the most recent Italian painting.
Rosenthal wrote the catalogue essay for
Paladino's London exhibition at Waddington
Galleries, in 1984 and also for this year's
exhibition, Mimmo Paladino: Black and White.
In his Italian Art in the Twentieth Century,
essay, Rosenthal described Paladino's thus:

*Paladino's eclecticism is characteristic of the
transavantguardia generation. For him, art
evokes secrets silently and functions in a
ritualistic way; the artist alone officiates
and we are merely privileged observers. His
paintings and sculpture, and his
remarkable drawings, are full of the
imagery of rituals; priests and witch doctors
engage in precisely those subterranean
dramas that exist in dreams and myths and
which in a post-Freudian age cannot be
satisfactorily explained. His works are not in
any sense programmatic. The ceremonial
banquets which are a recurring theme in his
work have a quality that evokes the notion of
death. They are literally 'natura morta', they
take one to a new reality in another world.
The figures are masked but the artist has
little wish to divulge their meaning.*[7]

Paladino describes his work in this way:
*The figures in my paintings, the animals,
the masks, the theme of death – I do not want
to explain or analyse them. They are the
roots out of which the picture develops, but
not its content. That is an entirely different
area which also cannot be researched with
the methods of art criticism. These things are
not decisive in the dispute between art and
the world. De Chirico never spoke
philosophically or psychoanalytically about
his work. He always said, 'I use colour, the
place, the painting of the Cinquecento, the
light, the surface'. This is how I wish to hear
painters talk about their work, not because I
believe art is a technical problem but
because the artist always plays his game of
hiding what might be evident.*[8]

Paladino is a master engraver and
printmaker. His graphic work (an etching is
included in the RA Summer Show) makes him
one of the most impressive printmakers working
today. The scale of the recent paintings, such as,
'Un Treno per Dulcinea', in the RA Summer
Exhibition is a masterpiece of scale and space. It
conjures a range of references, art historically –
Etruscan sculpture, Picasso, de Chirico, Joseph
Beuys. The wide range of references is
intriguing, The technical command of the space,
and the confidence with which he applies
blocks of colour, against a mostly black canvas,
and bold and resplendant use of gold leaf, owes
something to the great number of large-scale
drawings and prints he has made. Emancipated
from the realm of illustration, or using diaristic
entry, Paladino commands a large space with
his outstanding draughtsmanship. Drawing and
the graphic works are fundamental to his
painting. The relationship between words and
images is a central issue in many of his graphic

□ 4

works. The woodcuts and lino prints interact seamlessly with the paintings.

The grand yet sombre paintings on show in London are large in scale, using areas of black and gold leaf. References are made, to southern Italy where he continues to live and work, and to the layers of history, specifically Etruscan and Roman past. Benevento is steeped in Roman history, with one of the best preserved Roman arches in Italy dedicated to the Emperor Trajan, as well as one of the largest Roman theatres in existence, built by Hadrian and Caracalla. Paladino acknowledges the cultural strands that intertwine in this area of the south, as Rosenthal has aptly observed,

The Etruscan world flourished simultaneously with the highest period of Greek Mediterranean culture. From Greece the centre of that culture was to move gradually to Italy and over the centuries cultures built themselves on top of others with dizzying density; Christian Rome on top of Pagan Rome, the Goths, Vandals, Lombards, successively on top of Ancient Rome, reducing it through wars often to village status, the Normans from the north of Europe meeting up with Byzantine and even Islamic cultures, traces of which can indeed be found in Benevento in the twelfth century in cloisters of the Church of Santa

Sofia; the battles of Guelphs and Ghibelines, the Renaissance in all its glory and seemingly endless histories down to the disastrous vainglories of Fascism.[9]

The rejection of the transavantguardia in the 1980s by staunch modernists is in the light of the quality and variety of individual artists, somewhat dated. It can now, be viewed, as an inevitable reaction to the solipsistic conceptual art that had come to dominate the art scene at the time. The technical invention and originality in Mimmo Paladino's work puts him in a unique place in terms of his significance and importance. Above all else, the range of his work, the elegant visual language and the metaphysical content guarantees him a worthy position of one of Italy's finest living artists.

JMcK

References

1. Mimmo Paladino, quoted by Enzo Di Martino, *Mimmo Paladino Graphic Work, 1974–2001,* introduction by Klaus Albrecht Schöder, Rizzoli, New York: 4.
2. Norman Rosenthal, 'C.C.C.P.: Back to the Future', in *Italian Art of the Twentieth Century.* Painting and Sculpture, 1900-1988, Prestel with the Royal Academy, London, edited by Emily Braun, 1989, p.369.
3. Irving Sandler, *Art of the Post-Modern Era,* Icon Editions, Harper Collins, New York, 1996: 287.
4. Flash Art, quoted *ibid:* 288.
5. *Ibid:* 289.
6. *Ibid:* 289.
7. Rosenthal, 'Back to the Future', *op cit:* 372.
8. *Ibid:* 372.
9. Norman Rosenthal, *Mimmo Paladino, Black and White,* Waddington Galleries, London, 2006, p.6.

Word into Art: Artists of the Modern Middle East

The British Museum, London

18 May–3 September 2006

This beautiful exhibition of contemporary art from the Middle East and North Africa uses the written word as a common thread to draw together artists who incorporate script or scripture into their art in various ways, despite their geographically and culturally diverse traditions. The museum's acquisition policy has deliberately favoured works that complement its older collections of 'Islamic' art, but this does nothing to diminish the startling diversity and quality of work on show. If anything, it serves to underline the contemporary relevance of the region's literary and religious traditions.

A powerful illustration of this relevance can be seen in the Great Court. Here, Iraqi sculptor Dia al-Azzawi's 'Blessed Tigris' (2006) pushes its multicoloured fibreglass bulk into the air like an organic minaret. Inscribed around the base are lines by the modern Iraqi poet Muhammad Mahdi al-Jawahiri, written in the 1960s but resonating prophetically today:

> O wanderer, play with a gentle touch;
> Caress the lute softly and sing again,
> That you may soothe a volcano seething with rage
> And pacify a heart burning with pain.

Fittingly, the exhibition opens with a room dedicated to 'Sacred Script': it was the advent of Islam, and the need to record the text of the Qu'ran that galvanised the development of a written language for Arabic, and influenced the many calligraphic styles whose heritages these artists extend. The breadth of Islamic sacred tradition is well illustrated: this small room encompasses both Haji Noor Deen Mi Guanjiang's hanging scroll in the sini script of Chinese Muslim tradition, and Mouneer al-Shaarani's interpretation of a Biblical verse from Matthew, 'By their fruits ye shall know them', as well as work by Sudanese, Iraqi, Lebanese and Japanese artists.

The next room, 'Literature and Art', contains works that take as their point of departure secular texts, the rich and living traditions of pre-Islamic, Persian and Arabic poetry. Some artists, such as Hassan Massoudy, follow a long tradition of using calligraphy to illustrate verses. The painting that appears on the exhibition poster is his rendering of lines by the mystic poet Ibn 'Arabi (d.1240), loosely translated as:

> I follow the religion of Love
> Wherever its caravans head
> For Love is my religion and faith.

□ 1. Farhad Moshiri. *Drunken Lover*. Iran, 2005. © The artist/British Museum

□2

□3

4

Other artists approach the word not so much as bearer of lexical meaning to be embellished, but as a pure element of visual composition. Shirazeh Houshiary, an Iranian-born artist also known for her sculptures, is showing etchings of black overlapping circles on coloured fields. The shapes, reminiscent of molecules, solar systems, or the circular Dervish dance, are formed from the chants and prayers of the Sufi mystic Jalal al-Din Rumi, which have been overlaid until they become unreadable strokes. In the exhibition catalogue, the artist states that 'the word loses its meaning and form is born from this', a philosophy that echoes Rumi who wrote, 'when the body is shattered, the spirit lifts its head'.

The shattering of bodies – not as metaphor, but as daily political reality in Iraq, Lebanon and elsewhere – is a topic that many of the artists address, shoring the fragments of ancient cultures against the burned libraries, uranium-littered battlefields and looted museums of today. Suad al-Attar's Chagall-like figures float above lines by the early Arab poet Layla bint Lukayz (d.483): 'Sorrow alighted in my heart, and I melted / Even as lead melts when engulfed by flame'. Several of the artists, including al-Attar, live abroad – many in France, the US or the UK. At a time when the racist rhetoric of far-right parties is gaining support in Europe, their work testifies to the artistic rewards enjoyed by societies that welcome difference and don't force cultural homogeneity on their citizens.

Some of the most multi-layered and beautiful works in the exhibition are artists' books, including unique handmade objects, such as Etel Adnan's transcription of Nelly Salameh Amri's poem on the Lebanese Civil War, Blessed Day. Adnan has produced a Japanese-folded book, covered in Arabic script overlaid with lines and geometric symbols in watercolours reminiscent of Klee's Tunisian paintings. Other books are printed, such as Kamal Boullata's Beginnings, which juxtaposes English and Arabic versions of poems by the great contemporary Syrian/Lebanese poet Adonis with abstract colour fields that enhance the poems' moods. Elsewhere, the Algerian/French artist Rachid Koraïchi lends his distinct Maghribi illustrations to Mohammed Dib's poem on war and loss, L'enfant jazz: magical talismanic letter squares are interspersed with shapes derived from palms and doorways.

Separate rooms are dedicated to works that deconstruct script as a basis for abstract compositions, and to those that use text, often in the form of newsprint or graffiti, as a component in politically conscious works. A free leaflet provides translations of many of the poems, and a clear introduction to the traditional calligraphic scripts, in this excellent and timely exhibition. **JW**

1. *Roof penthouse*. Wolf D Prix, Helmut Swiczinsky and Partner, Vienna. Credit: Gerald Zugmann, Vienna

Sculptural Architecture from Austria

National Art Museum of China, Beijing

5–23 August 2006

Guangdong Museum of Art, Guangzhou

14 October–16 November 2006

This masterly exhibition has been organised with the support of, and in co-operation with, the Federal Chancellery of Austria and the Ministry of Culture of the People's Republic of China. It is the brainchild of the architect, Professor Hans Hollein, who curated it from Vienna in liaison with the Director of the National Art Museum of China, Beijing. It represents a long affair between Austria and China on cultural matters, and the Chinese authorities are to be complimented on their perspicacity and understanding for seeing it through. It follows an initial exhibition in Shanghai in 2001, covered by *Studio International.* Like its predecessor there, it is superbly designed and presented and is accompanied by an excellent catalogue, with Chinese and English texts, as well as a German-English edition; again the result of close collaboration between the two nations. Professor Jin Ling, as Chinese Co-ordinator, is due a special mention here. Key figures in the preparation and organisation were at the National Museum of China, Beijing, Director Fan Di'an, and at the Guangdong Museum of Art, Guangzhou, Director Wang Huangsheng.

The Chinese Minister of Culture, Sun Jiazheng, has always valued the creative aspect of architecture and building and the high esteem in which architecture has been held in China, both historically and in the 21st century.

Hans Hollein curated the exhibition himself, as the most distinguished practising architect and teacher in Austria, and for decades now a leading world figure in both architecture and visual arts. In his introduction to the catalogue, Hollein refers to a free-dimensionality in the architecture of space, which characterises the new architecture, but he also refers back to a past precedent. The focus on Austrian architecture, well illustrated in the catalogue, provides a survey of this precedent in Austria from the medieval to the baroque age, and a representative survey that then runs through the 19th and 20th centuries. This is followed by seven key sections, each devoted to a different aspect of the 21st-century architecture of Austria and including appropriate references to the developing links with China. For a small nation such as Austria, with a population of around eight million (compared to that of China's one thousand million), size has no

☐ 2

☐ 2. Hans Hollein. *Generali Media Tower,* Vienna, 2001. Credit: Archiv Hans Hollein, Vienna

☐ 3. *Pagoda in Nanjing.* 3rd book, A History of Architecture. Fischer von Erlach, JB. 60 x 42 cm, Vienna Museum. Credit: Vienna Museum

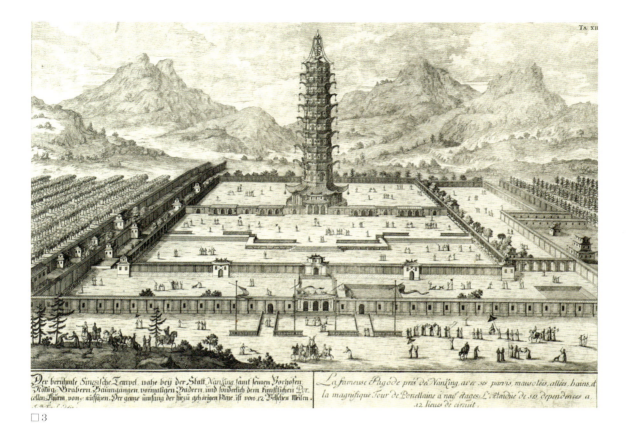

Der berühmte Sinesische Tempel, nahe bey der Statt Nanking samt seinen Vorhöfen, König: Gräbern, Baumgangen, vormaligen Pagoden, und sonderlich dem künstlichen Porcellan-Thurm von aussen. Der gantze umfang der hiezu gehörigen Plätze ist von 12 Welschen Meilen.

La fameuse Pagode près de Nanking, avec ses parvis, mausolées, allées, bains, d. la magnifique Tour de Porcellaine à neuf étages. L'étendüe de ses dependances a 12 lieues de circuit.

☐ 3

bearing on achievement in relative terms. There is evidence here of the degree to which, after decades of diplomatic and cultural exchange, all these initiatives are now at last bearing fruit, not only for Austria, but also Europe. It is also significant that Austria, as the key member of the Austro-Hungarian Empire (including what is now the Czech Republic, Slovakia and Hungary, as well as Austria) and China herself had in common the advantages and disadvantages of being empires. Recent commentators have referred to the extent to which Mao Tse-Tung is known to have admired so-called 'modern' architecture. His disregard for historical architecture was perhaps a result of ideological standpoints.

The sections on historical precedent here remind us of how the semantic, sculptural and cultural aspects of Viennese developments in architecture reflect on aspects of a city which became, like Paris, Florence and Rome, important as a centre of exchange for Europe as a whole. The question arises as to whether, in China or in Europe, cultural icons in

architecture, such as the Forbidden City, Beijing, or St Stephen's Cathedral, Vienna, can live in harmony with contemporary architecture. Quality in spatial disposition, design and 'placement' in relation to precedent and environment remains of the highest priority. This, perhaps, is the lesson that Austria carries to China, notably in Shanghai and Beijing. Hollein does not dwell on the area around St Stephen's Cathedral, yet in designing the Haas Haus shoppng centre and restaurant in the late 1980s, straight opposite the monument, he himself achieved an exemplary installation, totally complementary to the ancient cathedral. It is important in key locations to provide a complementary backdrop to the icons of the past, but not one that is self-effacing. Such lessons can only be proved by reality, on site. From baroque Vienna to the surge of opulent and expressive design of secessionist Vienna, as displayed at the turn of the 19th century, such issues were critical in the work of Otto Wagner and Adolf Loos. Next came the socialist housing of the Karl Marx Hof also in Vienna: before the surge of brilliant talent swept across to the USA, as exemplified by Schindler's Lovell Beach House in Los Angeles, and the contemporary house designed in central Vienna by the philosopher Ludwig Wittgenstein. The ensuing sculptural/architectural essays of buildings designed by Wilhelm Holzbauer, Walter Pichler, Gunther Domenig and Coop Himmelblau, all key motivators in the later 20th-century development of architectural thinking represent, for Chinese sensibilities, a genuinely experimental process, involving manifestos and discussions, which formed a turbulent period – a kind of cultural revolution by stealth. The product was the architectural wave, led by Hollein himself, which swept across Europe. In the 1970s, the buildings of Guenther Domenig and Hans Hollein shook conventional foundations to the core.

A nation such as China cannot fail to be inspired by European works like 'Volcania', the new European Volcanology Park in France, by Hans Hollein (won in a major competition), as they search there for new concepts to house their own superb collections from history. The continuing fluidity and sculptural diversity of contemporary Austrian architects has struck a chord in Shanghai, Beijing and Guangzhou, and will duly help in the liberalisation of deep-frozen ideas in China. Maximilian Fuchsas and the British designer, Zaha Hadid, are also included in the survey in respect of their work in China, offering new interpretations of the typology of 'blocks'. The buildings of the Americans Greg Lynn and Steven Holl have also deserted the mainstream vulgarity of American ad mass design in all its complacency and materialism, providing visitor and interpretation centres that open the eyes. In rapidly expanding Chinese cities, Dominique Perrault's re-interpretation of the 'point block' formula itself can inspire future builders and developers in China.

A separate section of the exhibition focuses on the opportunities posed in Austria of the single-family house, which may well take on a new life in China. Yet a further section of the exhibition is devoted to the works of Austrian architects Rainer Pirker, already engaged with Chinese clients, or in competitions there. The 'Heaven's Seal Culture Club' proposed for Nanjing offers new solutions to the intricate question of buildings in relation to their close surroundings, and what is 'site' and what is 'non-site' in a hilly topography. Rainer was himself earlier a special advocate of the form of Chinese cities, in his book *The World as a Garden – China*, with its particular focus on courtyard houses there.

This exhibition comes as special witness for those outside the China 'loop', of how a determined but confident Austria has penetrated Chinese traditional cultural preserves and reservations, and opened a mutually beneficial creative dialogue. This is now leading on to significant construction projects, as well as to greater mutual understanding between Austria and China about what really constitutes sculptural architecture, itself the apotheosis of blandness. In the European engagement with China, Austria is, by stealth and diplomacy as well as enlightened talent, now in pole position.
Editor

AngloMania: Tradition and Transgression in British Fashion

The Metropolitan Museum of Art, New York

3 May–4 September 2006

Attracting those amorous of Englishness, the socialites and libertines who wear Westwood so well, the Metropolitan Museum of Art's 'AngloMania' exhibition this summer has featured internationally in haute couture magazines of the fashionable. Capturing an impression of a nation's notorious vanity, a romance with itself, and the eccentric desire of English designers to re-establish the establishment, the Metropolitan presents quite an odd phenomenon: the Englishness the Western world knows through myth and condescending glances – the notion of a nation.

The myth began once upon a time in the midst of the Enlightenment, when England was perceived as 'a land of reason, freedom, and tolerance' and drove Voltaire to exclaim, 'If ever I come a second time on Earth, I will pray God to make me born in England, the Land of Liberty'. Presumably, he was happy enough that his first life on earth was set in France, though, and one can see why from the little Francomania accessory to the wider exhibition in the 'Croome Court Room, Worcestershire,

c.1771', which shows tapestries woven at the royal Gobelins Manufactory in Paris. This Earl's wife had a fetish for all things français, and enjoyed wearing couture from the marchands de modes on the rue Saint-Honoré, pieces of which drape the mannequins. The roots of modern French influence in British fashion are traced back to the House of Worth, whose clothes were characterised by Parisian elegance, the romance of France romanticised further by the dreams and ideals of the British designers. These days, British designer, John Galliano, follows the pattern by designing the Dior collection and, in so doing, translates the Paris he perceives with the outsider's subjective romanticism into frills and fun of the highest order. England and France have traditionally played games of vanity with one another, especially in the 18th century: the English wore idealistic couture of the French, and the French wore Anglomanic creations in turn. They waltz together in a ballroom decorated with mirrors, and as they dance, they catch their own reflections in the mirrored décor, slightly more

□ 1. *Jacket,* 1996–97. Union Jack jacket designed by Alexander McQueen in collaboration with David Bowie, using distressed fabric. Worn by David Bowie on the Earthling album tour, 1996-97. Collection of David Bowie.

1

2

2. Vivienne Westwood. *Queen-ish Ensemble* (British, b. 1941). Harris Tweed collection autumn/winter 1987–88. Burgundy cotton velvet with blue wool piping; faux ermine fur; black leather and natural wood; faux ermine fur and multicolored felted wool crown. Los Angeles County Museum of Art, Costume Council Fund, M.2002.97a-f. Photography © 2002 Museum Associates/LACMA

interested in the spectacle they create with each turn, rather than each other. They court one another, that is all.

The court, of course, is the game at play here. It has shifted setting – from the palace to the Metropolitan – but it remains the same. As displayed by such princesses and eccentrics of the modern age, including Kate Moss, Vivienne Westwood, Lindsey Lohan, Sarah Jessica Parker, Sophie Dahl and Sienna Miller at the Costume Institute Ball, the art gallery is New York's answer to the palace – or at least one of its answers – and, appropriately, that is where its 'royalty' court the attention of the press. New York has invited England to the Metropolitan - a lovely exchange from one island to another - and 'AngloMania' is a kiss-kiss as part of their romantic bond.

English wit sparkles in the conversation and commentary, and New York responds with a fluttering giggle. Part of the joke is that although France is mentioned in a little Francomania vignette of the museum, it is dismissed rather than embraced, and there really aren't that many French people around. France and England have always acted as each other's particular companions in the world's masquerade, but it seems from this exhibition that New York has stolen England's affections for a while. In the wider world of fashion and society, New York and England now share a closer bond than England and France. Society girls would rather flick through American Vogue for an education in manners than actually have to learn grammar. Shoes or verbs? That is the question. The pretty shoes hardly touch the ground for all the dancing they do.

'AngloMania' is the obsession with Englishness – although a fever provoked by grounded realities is a mania mostly of the mind, a fever of nerves, a pretty madness, a fictive flourish ... Englishness is a myth, a mutual fantasy whose ideals are attune with one another. As 'The Hunt Ball' section suggests, British style and couture also react to political dramas, gelling in seductive antagonism with the mannequins bearing punk-ish attire, shouting that whether in high society or low society, subversion is the fun to be had. The central irony of British fashion, and British society at large, is that the factions possess the same style, the same glare and the same pout, inherent in all the fox fur and chains of generations.

Whether for a punk or a princess, British fashion is much more than frills and frolics; it encompasses every nuance of the masquerade and rebellion ongoing in British society at every level, excluding perhaps the bourgeoisie. Britishness, that self-affirming glance in the mirror at one's undeniable beauty, is a reaction to the horrible rain, the nauseating shade of grey the sky insists on wearing and those mean dregs of humanity who just have a thing against the upper classes. It is make-up and make-believe painted prettily on the face of adversity. It is a gin-in-teacups and mud-on-lace kind of style that attracts Anglophiles as the years roll by, and shows no sign of ever going out of vogue. The myth will not be dismissed. The myth is here to stay, because New York says it is. Kiss kiss. **CS**

Rodin

Royal Academy of Arts, London

23 September 2006–1 January 2007

The Royal Academy is currently thronged with jostling human bodies and body parts. These are not, however, composed of the flesh and blood of the great art-going public, but are inanimate bits and figures, all in the name of Auguste Rodin, the great French sculptor, who died in 1917.

We cannot cease to be reminded of Rodin, because he seemed to provide the jumping-off point for so many of the leading artists of the remainder of the 20th century. Matisse, for example, had a supposedly formative meeting with Rodin in 1900, in his studio. At that juncture, Rodin's reputation was long formed as the great individual who had given new life to an art form that had atrophied. Matisse's curiosity related chiefly to Rodin's sculptural method and practice as such, and less so in terms of his drawing technique. So Matisse's contemporary figure sculpture 'The Serf' (1900–03) was doubtless executed under the particular influence of Rodin, yet it also epitomises Matisse's own determined breach from any attempt to emulate Rodin's practice.

While Matisse therefore seemed ultimately to dismiss Rodin's method of disjunctive application of 'bit parts' in his work, Brancusi, who served only a four-week stint in Rodin's studio as one of over 40 at work there, came to accept Rodin's 'cut and paste' practice, the moving and detaching of fragments large and small for the greater good of any particular sculpture in priority over the others. But for Brancusi, such proximity to this gigantic reputation was too close for comfort – he left after four weeks, having absorbed the message.

The exhibition at the Royal Academy, which has just opened, has caught the notorious congestion of the Rodin Museum in Paris, and yet in the aggrandisement and monumentalisation of the figures that are, so to say, whole entities, something of the immediacy of the Rodin Museum is inevitably lost here. The figures themselves are invariably distorted (with the exception of the early work), exaggerated in the awkwardness of their poses. This fragmentation on a massive scale is not alleviated but increased by the wealth of

☐ 1. Auguste Rodin. *The Kiss,* 1901–04. Marble 182.2 x 121.9 x 153 cm. Tate, London, NO6228. Photo © Tate, London 2006

☐ 2. Auguste Rodin. *Le Poète et la Sirène (La Vague).* Bronze 12.5 x 25 x 13 cm City Council, Glasgow, No. 7.9. Photo © Glasgow City Council (Museums)

□ 1

□ 2

□ 3

documentation provided: period photographs, images of the great man at work and prints of some of the great 'stuffed-shirt' commemorative banquets laid on in England and France, all go to emphasise the gravitas and greatness of France's pre-eminent sculptor. The ambivalent photographic array of female images, ranging from erotic sepia nudes, from humble but flirtatiously provocative models to taunting, flattering well-corseted grandes dames is, one might say, a useful adjunct to the show. From the sublime (Gwen John in the nude) to the ridiculous (George Bernard Shaw posing nude as 'the Thinker') there is a full exposé.

Is Rodin overwhelming? Or to today's distinctly jaundiced eye – from that of Tracey Emin to Damien Hirst – somewhat underwhelming in the final analysis? Was it all too much? In the show, the total accumulation of 'bits and pieces' somehow diminishes the masterworks. For the 21st century, too, the longer-term critical fallout might seem to be distinctly over extended. The great masters of the 20th century, such as Brancusi, but also Moore, certainly seem to owe less and less to Rodin, except to have escaped to work another day, another mode. Rodin was the master of 'recombinant' sculpture. In connecting and reconnecting different human part sculptures, within reach of his studio, like some atavistic archaeologist, moving from work on one half-finished sculpture to another and back again, Rodin established a fundamental working

3. Auguste Rodin. *The Thinker,* 1884.
Bronze 71.4 x 59.9 x 42.2 cm. National Gallery of Victoria,
Melbourne, Australia, Felton Bequest, 1921, 1196_3.
Photo © NGV Photographic Services

4. Auguste Rodin. *St John the Baptist,* 1879.
Bronze 200 x 120 x 56 cm Victoria and Albert Museum,
London, 601-1092. Photo © V&A Images/V&A Museum

process for the benefit of all sculptors of the 20th century and beyond. Recombinant – the ability to combine and recombine divergent yet selected elements all the time in an ongoing process – that was Rodin's great innovation. It could be said that Henry Moore, Antony Caro, Bill Tucker, even Alberto Giacometti and Eduardo Paolozzi and not least Antony Gormley, all gained from this process as legitimised by Rodin, to a greater or lesser degree – and it percolated through the schools of sculpture and through the generations. Then each and all got the hell out of it: Rodin was too all embracing, as the multitalented Michael Ayrton was sadly to discover.

Rodin's Balzac must, however, remain one of the great individual 20th century monuments. Likewise, the remarkable group sculpture, 'The Burghers of Calais', stands today as a triumph of figurative art. Here, one is reminded directly of Rodin's very early bronze figure entitled 'The Age of Bronze' (1877). As time went on Rodin became increasingly preoccupied by female models, whom he could draw without ever dropping his penetrating gaze from their beguiling forms. It is ironic, therefore, that Rodin gave street credibility to the plagiarising and appropriation of form taken from the work of other artists, or ancient precedents. Rodin's 'borrowings' seem to be little disguised, and so readily identifiable for the most part. And so perhaps this among other skills is what makes Rodin, essentially 'recombinant' sculptor as he was, a precursor to 21st century art.

Editor

4

Francis Bacon in the 1950s

Sainsbury Centre for Visual Arts, Norwich

26 September–10 December 2006

The Sainsbury Centre for Visual Arts seems like a fitting starting point for this fascinating touring exhibition. During the early part of Francis Bacon's career, the collectors Robert and Lisa Sainsbury provided crucial support to the artist as friends, patrons and, eventually, as financial guarantors, and the 13 works that they purchased in the 1950s provide a valuable foundation for this show, which sheds new light on the development of the painter's practice.

In the exhibition catalogue, Michael Peppiatt, Bacon's biographer and guest curator of the exhibition, describes the 1950s as the period in which Bacon 'came of age as a painter'.[1] However, this was by no means a time of contemplative development for the artist: homeless, saddled with debt and caught up in a tempestuous relationship with Peter Lacy, Bacon's peripatetic existence could have put a great strain on his ability to work. Nevertheless, Peppiatt portrays this time as the most richly inventive period of Bacon's career, drawing an analogy between these 'Wanderjahre'[2] and the artist's search for the appropriate subject matter and technique with which to express himself fully.

Concentrating as it does on this key period in the artist's life, the show cannot help but have a certain biographical emphasis, and Peppiatt's catalogue essay, peppered with anecdotes, acknowledges the continuing fascination that Bacon's life story inspires. However, the selection of work brought together here is no less fascinating. During his lifetime, Bacon was an exacting self-critic, who destroyed, 'lost' and re-bought paintings that he felt were deficient or for which he developed a dislike. Yet it seems that sufficient time has elapsed since Bacon's death in 1992 for Peppiatt to look beyond the standardised canon that the artist fostered, showing works that Bacon would not necessarily have included in a retrospective.

The curator has also sought to illustrate the working processes behind Bacon's oeuvre by displaying some of the archival material, which became available after Bacon's death. In the 'Link' section of the gallery, between the two exhibition spaces, visitors can see an assortment of visual materials recovered from Bacon's London studio by conservators from the Hugh Lane Gallery, including photographs, book plates and magazine cuttings, and a number of drawings lent by Tate. However, Peppiatt has to admit that 'all the sources in the world ... will never do more than illuminate the matrix out of which a powerful work of art has emerged'.[3] Rather, it is the simultaneous presentation of 50 paintings, including some rarely seen works, which provide the viewer with a detailed insight into Bacon's artistic preoccupations during the 1950s and beyond.

The first room of the exhibition provides an overview of the wide range of subjects that Bacon painted during this decade and it is interesting to see early portraits and familiar

□ 1

□ 1. Francis Bacon. *Study of a Nude,* 1952–3. Oil on canvas 59.7 x 49.5cm. Robert and Lisa Sainsbury Collection

2

□ 3

□ 2. Francis Bacon. *Portrait of Lisa,* 1956. Oil on canvas 100.6 x 72.7 cm. Robert and Lisa Sainsbury Collection

□ 3. Francis Bacon. *Portrait of Lisa,* 1957. Oil on canvas 59.7 x 49.5 cm. Robert and Lisa Sainsbury Collection

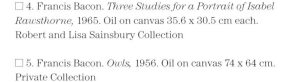

☐ 4. Francis Bacon. *Three Studies for a Portrait of Isabel Rawsthorne,* 1965. Oil on canvas 35.6 x 30.5 cm each. Robert and Lisa Sainsbury Collection

☐ 5. Francis Bacon. *Owls,* 1956. Oil on canvas 74 x 64 cm. Private Collection

studies after Velázquez's 'Pope Innocent X' exhibited next to rare paintings of animals and landscapes. 'Owls' (1956) and 'Figure with Monkey' (1951) are quietly unsettling figurative studies, while 'Elephant Fording a River' (1952) and 'Figure in a Landscape' (1957) explode with uncharacteristic colour and movement. The startling 'Study for a Portrait of van Gogh V' (1957) shows its eponymous subject in a brightly coloured natural setting, casting a strong shadow on the path behind him. This creates a sense of depth, which appears remarkable to viewers more familiar with the claustrophobic interiors of his other work. At the same time however, Bacon was also producing images like 'Study for a Figure VI' (1956–57) showing a man framed by a low ceiling, and the beautiful 'Study of a Nude' (1952–53); a delicate figure suspended or poised to dive at the edge of an imagined space rendered in black, blue and white.

The second room of the show contains a number of portraits and figure studies from the later 50s and early 60s, while the inclusion of 'Three Studies for a Portrait of John Edwards', from 1984, shows where this work would eventually lead. While the selection of paintings on show here is perhaps less surprising than in the first room, it is still a rich and enjoyable one, with works such as 'Seated Figure' (1961) showing the coming together of Bacon's earlier compositional and technical investigations. Bacon saw painting as 'a mysterious and continuous struggle with chance',[4] and his frequent return to certain subjects yielded a wide stylistic variety. Two variations that

demonstrate his range are the portraits of Lisa Sainsbury, which are normally dispersed among the Sainsbury Centre's collection. In the 1956 'Portrait of Lisa', Bacon has laid the paint on and then scraped it off, so that the subject is barely present on the canvas, while in the version dated 1957, the paint is laid on so thickly round the eyes and forehead that her face becomes a moulded and gouged mask. This latter approach to portraiture appears again in Bacon's studies from the 1960s of his friends, Isabel Rawsthorne and Lucian Freud. Here, the heavy swirl and strike of the paint transforms brows, noses and mouths into snouts, muzzles, tusks and markings, the primal reading of expression obscuring the figurative appearance of the face beneath.

This invigorating exhibition, which will travel to Milwaukee and Buffalo in 2007, provides a thorough account of Francis Bacon's early practice. It reveals the strength of the Sainsbury Centre's own collection of Bacon works and, in focusing on the 1950s, shows the painter at his most open and experimental, in the process of becoming the iconic artist whose paintings still challenge and compel us today. The exhibition travels to Milwaukee Art Museum, Wisconsin, USA, from 29 January–15 April 2007 and then to the Albright-Knox Art Gallery, Buffalo, USA, from 5 May–30 July 2007. **SD**

References
1. Peppiatt M. *Francis Bacon in the 1950s.* Norwich: Sainsbury Centre for Visual Art, 2006: 14.
2. *Ibid:* 16.
3. *Ibid:* 10–11.
4. *Ibid:* 46.

☐ 4

☐ 5

Leonardo da Vinci: Experience, Experiment, Design

Victoria and Albert Museum, London

14 September 2006–7 January 2007

☐ 1. Leonardo da Vinci. *Vertical and horizontal sections of the human head and eye*, c.1489. Pen and ink and red chalk, 20.3 x 14.3 cm. Royal Collection © 2006 Her Majesty Queen Elizabeth II

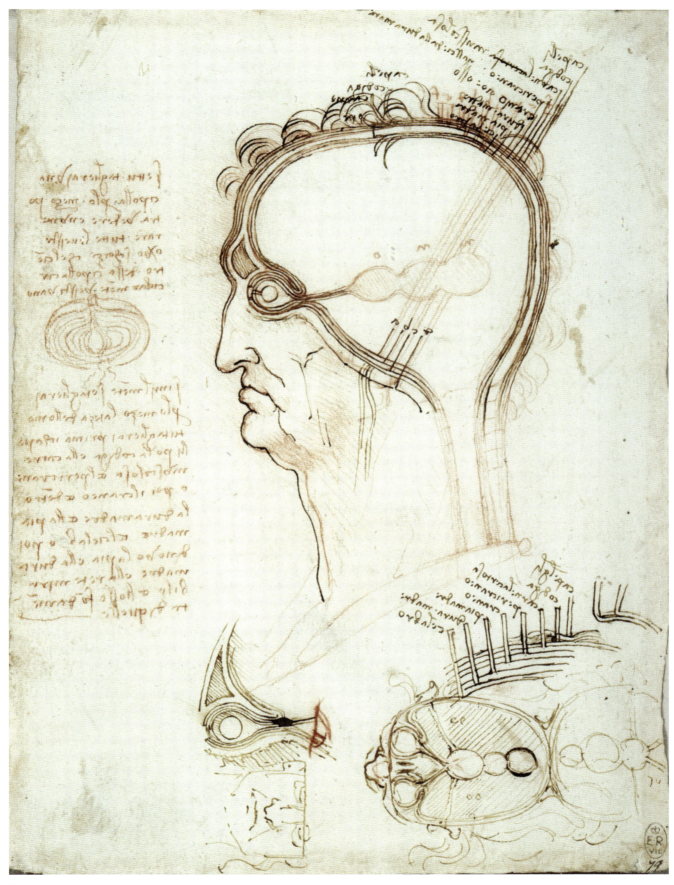

1

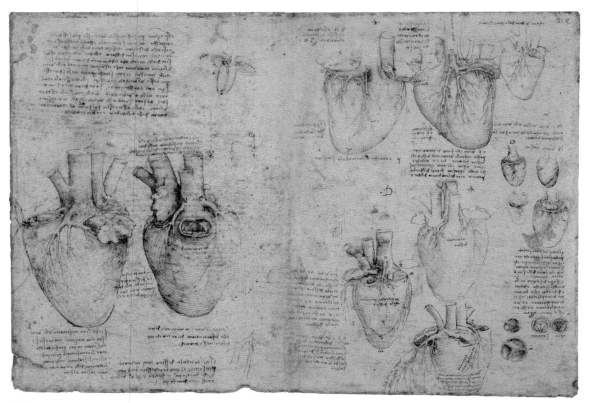

□ 2

No major painter in the history of art has a surviving corpus of paintings smaller than that of Leonardo da Vinci. Only a handful of paintings remain, some unfinished, some of disputed attribution, and at least one of the most significant in a grievous state of decay which commenced shortly after it was completed. Ask most otherwise culturally informed people to name some paintings by Leonardo, and they will probably come up with no more than three: 'Mona Lisa', 'Madonna of the Rocks' and 'The Last Supper'. Moreover, in comparison with other major painters with a relatively small oeuvre such as Vermeer, Leonardo's agreed surviving works exhibit a perplexing diversity of style and execution.

One is entitled to ask why, in this case, Leonardo holds a position of such remarkable pre-eminence in the history of Western art. The answer can be found in the drawings and notes presented in this exhibition – his prodigious and unparalleled output as a thinker, scientist, inventor and designer. The work gathered together here exhibits an almost frightening and inexhaustible curiosity, and a mental energy that ranged over every phenomenon capable of scientific empirical enquiry.

These included, first and foremost, the form and function of the human body. As a topic for study, the human form had a special and pre-eminent significance in Leonardo's age. Most artists would have been led to it primarily as a source of imagery in painting, sculpture and design, capable of expressing the most profound and subtle aspects of the human condition. Mastering the depiction of the human form meant acquiring the ability to express and convey complex spiritual states, emotion and action. For the practising artist in an age of homocentric imagery it was a sine qua non in the production not only of religious commissions, but the satisfaction of the

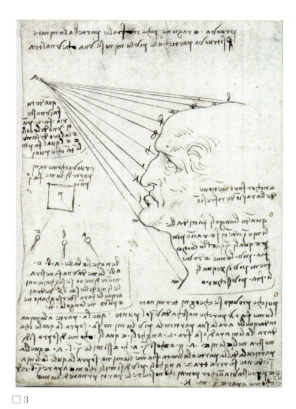

□ 3

□ 4

□ 2. Leonardo da Vinci. *Studies of the heart of an ox*, c.1513. Pen and ink on blue paper, 28 x 41 cm. Royal Collection © 2006 Her Majesty Queen Elizabeth II

□ 3. Leonardo da Vinci. *Head of a man showing how rays of light fall upon the face from an adjacent source*, c.1488. Pen and ink on white paper, 20.3 x 14.3 cm. Royal Collection © 2006 Her Majesty Queen Elizabeth II

□ 4. Leonardo da Vinci. *Men at work, digging, carrying, pulling etc*, c.1509. Black chalk with some pen, 20.1 x 13 cm. Royal Collection © 2006 Her Majesty Queen Elizabeth II

□ 5. Leonardo da Vinci. *Deluge with rocks, floods and a tree*, c.1516. 15.8 x 20.3 cm. Royal Collection © 2006 Her Majesty Queen Elizabeth II

□ 5

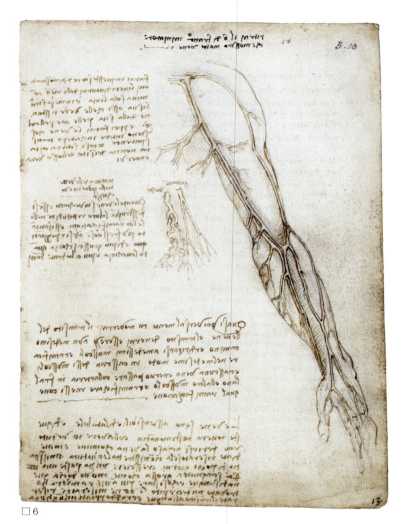

□ 6

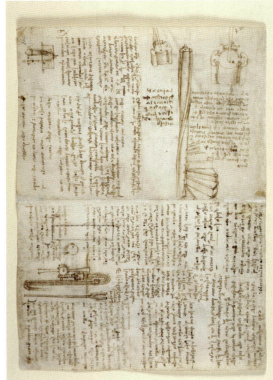

□ 8

□ 7

□ 6. Leonardo da Vinci. *Vessels of the arm with comparison of vessels in the old and the young,* c.1508. Pen and ink, 19 x 13.3 cm. Royal Collection © 2006 Her Majesty Queen Elizabeth II

□ 7. Leonardo da Vinci. *Studies of horses and horsemen for the Battle of Anghiari,* c.1503. Pen and Ink, 8.3 x 12 cm. The British Museum, London

□ 8. Leonardo da Vinci. *Studies of a spiral staircase and of a pump,* c.1514. 28 x 18 cm (page size in bound volume). British Library, London

□ 9. Leonardo da Vinci. *Man Climbing a Ladder,* c.1494. Code Forster II. 19.5 x 7 cm. Victoria and Albert Museum, London

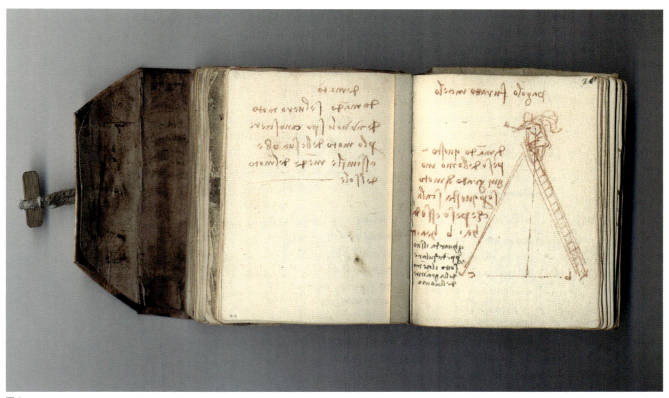

□9

burgeoning appetite for Classical subjects and, within Leonardo's lifetime, a growing market for secular subjects with no particular moral, religious or historical significance.

It is often remarked, in regard to art preceding the 19th century, that it pre-dated the invention of photography. The implication is that handcrafted productions in the form of drawings and designs are inevitably inferior to what could eventually be achieved with a camera. Leonardo's drawings expose the profound misconception behind this widely held presumption. No camera has ever, or will ever, provide us with a more vivid picture of, for example, the disposition of the internal organs of the human form than that provided in Leonardo's drawings. This is a conclusion vindicated by fact that even today, in the age of high-quality colour digital photography, contemporary medical artists still fall back on hand-rendered images to capture and communicate complex and subtle medical and

surgical information. Compared with the human eye and the human hand, the camera is and will remain a relatively crude instrument for recording visual facts.

Leonardo's preoccupation with the physical world around him had three aspects: retrospective, prospective and speculative. In retrospective mode, he looked back upon inherited physical reality and attempted to analyse and record what presented itself to his senses. Hence we find the painstaking records of the nature and function of the human form, the structure of the skeleton, the disposition and operation of organs, the oddities of physiognomy, and so on. In the same vein of enquiry we have countless drawings that attempt to understand the form, nature and movement of all physical phenomena, including the more amorphous ones such as water and air.

In prospective mode, Leonardo used his newly acquired knowledge to imagine how an understanding of these phenomena might be exploited in the invention and development of things not yet in existence, such as flying machines, civil engineering projects, new building forms and weapons systems.

In what I have called speculative mode, he moved beyond the recording of existing phenomena and the projection of new inventions in the pursuit of an overarching theoretical system that would bring both together in one grand scientific explanatory scheme; hence his interest in mathematics and geometry.

Leonardo was born in what we might still call with justification the Middle Ages; he died in what we rightly call the High Renaissance. His turbulent and, at times, painful journey from one to the other reflects at a personal level what was happening in Western society in general. It was an age when most of the comforting but stagnant assumptions that dominated the medieval world were challenged and then overthrown by new scholarship and new aspirations. One driving force behind this development was the rediscovery of Classical science, literature and culture. Leonardo belonged to that generation of artists who were no longer content with the cultural and social status of a humble technician, simply interpreting, realising and executing the requests and wishes of his clients, like a conscientious craftsman constructing a piece of furniture to order. He demanded and was granted a cultural status comparable with that of the philosopher, the poet and the statesman.

He realised that he did not possess, and never would acquire, some of the skills and attributes that were, in his day, regarded as the prerequisites of someone cultivated in the liberal arts. He never gained more than a rudimentary competence in Latin, at that time regarded as what we now call an essential 'core skill'. It is also, I understand, possible to fault some of his mathematics. However, in Leonardo's day there were literally countless well-educated men of learning who could throw off an elegant stanza in Latin and had mastered Euclid from beginning to end. They have disappeared into the oblivion of history. Leonardo has not, because he possessed to a prodigious degree other skills of much greater significance; notably the ability to perceive, to record, to examine, to think and to speculate.

His example and his message for us today is that one must never be content with received wisdom, whether in the form of science, technology or social practice. The society that convinces itself that everything which needs to be known is known, and that the way things are done is the best of all possible ways, is a society in stagnation, and will ultimately die on its feet. Leonardo's greatest attribute, which underpins all his achievements as an artist and thinker, was that he did not take anything for granted. This is the fact that emerges most forcibly from his work and from this exhibition. **CA**

☐ 10

□ 1

□ 1. *Installation view*. Frieze Art Fair, 2006

□ 2. Tom Claassen, *'Rabbits': Two Rabbits,* 2004 © Linda Nylind, courtesy Frieze Art Fair.

2

Frieze Art Fair 2006

Regent's Park, London

12–15 October 2006

The Frieze Art Fair is many things: a spectacle, a film festival, a four-day extravaganza of talks, tours and projects. Primarily though, it is an opportunity to buy and sell art, and it excels at this, with sales profits of £33 million last year. But what, if anything, lies beyond and behind its commercial glamour?

This question seems to have exercised several of the artists commissioned by Frieze Projects this year. Mike Nelson's installation, 'Mirror Infill', took the fairgoer behind the glamour in a literal sense, through an unmarked door and into an alternative labyrinthine world that snaked through a hidden space between the gallery stands. It inverted the rules of the fair: aseptic white walls were replaced by dusty workrooms and abandoned institutional corridors, bright lights exchanged for the shadowy red of a dark room, the green glow of an exit sign, or a low-wattage extension bulb in its metal cage. The detritus that littered the benches and floor was that of an obsessive photographer, and pegged to lines across the low ceiling were hundreds of photos of the marquee under construction, ranging from piles of scaffolding to shots of the almost-finished temporary galleries.

Loris Gréaud, in collaboration with DGZ Research, furnished Frieze with an exhibition of nano-sculptures, invisible to the naked eye. This project was called 'Why Is a Raven Like a Writing Desk?', the title taken from the riddle without an answer that Lewis Carroll's Mad Hatter poses Alice in Alice in Wonderland. Just as Carroll's conundrum assumes there is a connection, and challenges the reader to suppose otherwise, so Gréaud's small exhibition was determined by the conviction that these invisible objects were actually there. As the sculptures were only a few micrometers across, there was no recourse to an 'independent' verification procedure, and the viewer had to accept that the theatre of gallery assistants, catalogues, dramatic lighting and stylish black display stands actually had a purpose. Disruption of scale is an effective technique for questioning received ideas, and this project prompted questions about the importance of the context in which a work of art appears. Sometimes, Gréaud seemed to be saying, the context can eclipse the work itself, even stand in for it.

Of course, this analysis is only appropriate if the art in question is an object, a tangible thing that can be given a price tag and shipped off around the world to an international buyer. The interesting thing about this year's commissioned works is that many of them weren't commodities, and so provided a suitable counterpoint to the objects in the commercial gallery stands. The excellent Resonance 104.4 fm (www.resonancefm.com) was again broadcasting on-site from a soundproofed booth, available to anyone who managed to catch the transmissions as they disappeared into the ether. Joanna Callaghan and Russell Martin, whose previous productions for the radio station have included 'Show Me the Monet',[1] a series of conversations about art and economy's interactions, returned to this theme with two broadcasts entitled 'For Love & Money',[2] for

□ 3

□ 3. *Installation view.* Frieze Art Fair, 2006

□ 4

which they commissioned artists to work with ideas raised in the earlier series. I asked the two organisers about their intentions in programming the shows. Callaghan replied:

I really wanted to utilise the framework of the fair and the economic model that underpins such an event to produce 'product' that would never be sold. Hence, we commissioned artists to make work, though we gave little in the way of a brief. Since we could not pay the artists or sell their work in any conventional sense of the word, this allowed us to bypass notions of 'quality', saleability or value and explore a methodology of relations devoid of economic power, but which was situating itself inside an event entirely constructed around such power relations. A little bit of utopian rebelliousness perhaps.[3]

For Martin, it was important 'to work with other practitioners to present a unified or cumulative voice, or at least work towards one. [...] In this way, we can avoid the complaining tone often witnessed in the visual arts - not getting paid enough money, not getting enough

□ 4. *Installation view*. Frieze Art Fair, 2006

□ 5. Richard Deacon, *'Masters': Masters of the Universe: Screen Version,* 2005 © Linda Nylind, courtesy Frieze Art Fair

5

exposure, not finding support for non-material practices – and instead present our arguments and concerns cogently and intelligently to whoever happens to tune in. We can begin to talk.'

In terms of both visitor numbers and sales, Frieze is huge. The fair's organisers, Amanda Sharp and Matthew Slotover, revealed that they expected upwards of 10,000 visitors on the invite-only preview day alone. I asked the broadcasters for their take on this financial gigantism, and whether they thought it distorted public perception of art. According to Martin:

Without the phenomenal financial success of the YBAs and later artists, the visibility of the visual arts in this country would probably still be in a parlous state. But commercial activity is only a small part of what art used to be about - now a general perception that all artists earn huge sums of money from their practice has bred a kind of mistrust between people who practice art and those who don't, further removing art from the 'real world' whereas, in actual fact, art is as much a part of lived

experience as beans on toast [...] A friend recently told me he was talking to a London cabbie in his cab who, rather than ask 'What do you make?' when told my friend is an artist, asked 'Where do you show?' It's arguable which is the more sophisticated response - a mindset that states artists all make something, or one that thinks those things are always exhibited.

Yet Callaghan enjoyed the fair for its spectacular quality. 'Most of us were not there to buy work, we were there for the spectacle and I felt pleased for those artists and curators and gallerists who were able to profit from the event. Why shouldn't they?'

Both agreed that their critique concerned the system of which Frieze is a part, rather than Frieze per se. And it's certainly true that a lot of interesting work was on show at this year's fair, presented as always as part of a dizzying panoply of discussions, films, installations, consumption and display. Yet in this abundance of stimuli, a few works still stood out. Victoria Miro was showing one of Conrad Shawcross's large kinetic sculptures, which hummed and clicked a syncopated rhythm as its articulated

☐ 6

☐ 7

☐ 8

wooden arms spun lit bulbs in complex, fairground loops. Do-Ho Suh, known for his full-scale recreations of domestic architecture in translucent artificial fabrics, had two works installed at the Lehmann Maupin stand. 'Floor' (1997–2005) consisted of glass plates supported by thousands of tiny plastic human figures, packed together and with their hands raised, Atlas-like, to the glass above them. This floor was surrounded on four sides by 'Screen' (2004), a mesh wall constructed from similar plastic figures, cast in a rainbow of colours and joined at hands and feet into a chain-link of X-shapes. Doggerfisher was screening a collaboration between Rosalind Nashashibi and Lucy Skaer, 'Flash in the Metropolitan' (2006). Shot at night in the New York Metropolitan Museum of Art, this short film revealed display cases of objects from Africa and Oceania, briefly illuminated by a flash bulb. Dramatic shadows and intense reflections of polished metal grew and then withdrew into darkness again, in a rhythm as ceaseless as the sea.

The five short films commissioned for the 'Artists Cinema' this year were also interesting. Manon de Boer, a Dutch artist living in Brussels, produced 'Presto - Perfect Sound', which showed the composer and violinist George Van Dam performing part of a Bartók violin sonata. The soundtrack was edited from several takes to perfect continuity, whereas the musician's head and shoulders occasionally jumped sideways on screen. The fierce concentration on Van Dam's face, his occasional flourishes and inadvertent twitches, together with the rich musical tones, made for a compulsive cinematic experience.

Miguel Calderón's 'Guest of Honor' provided viewers with a mysterious short story, in which a family found a deer in the woods, and brought this symbol of wildness into their home. Meanwhile, Glasgow-based artist, Phil Collins, produced 'he who laughs last laughs longest', a documentary record of a laughing contest he set up in the US. Contestants competed for a cash prize by laughing continuously for as long as they could, eventually giving up in despair. All the commissions will eventually tour UK cinemas, showing before main features.

If the frenzy of the marquee became overwhelming, there were several avenues of escape: outside to the sculpture park perhaps, to wander between Tom Claassen's huge plastic rabbits, or gaze at Berta Fischer's complex folds of Perspex, or Roman Signer's kayak thrust into a pyramid of gravel. The talks offered escape of another sort, with some excellent speakers. I caught Liam Gillick proposing a series of 'findings' on contemporary art, and listened to an engaging debate on performance-based art chaired by Claire Bishop and broadcast live by Resonance (as were all the talks). Frieze may be commercially minded, but it has become a place where debate can flourish, and, thanks to the annual commissions, a place where non-commercial ventures can reach a wider audience. **JW**

References
1. www.showmethemonet.org.uk (last accessed 23 October 2006)
2. www.forloveandmoney.org.uk (last accessed 23 October 2006)
3. All quotations from personal email communication with the author, 17 October 2006.

Ettore Sottsass: Architect & Designer

Ronald T Labaco. London & New York: Merrell, 2006. ISBN 18589943205

Perhaps the most surprising statement in this book (at least for a European) is that Ettore Sottsass is still virtually unknown in the USA. This despite the shock and horror of 'Memphis' (and the film parodying its style, 'Ruthless People', starring Danny De Vito and Bette Midler), the work of ex-Memphis designer Peter Shire in California, and the fact that Sottsass himself designed the GE115 computer, which was made jointly by Olivetti, Bull in France and General Electric in America in 1967. There is also the Murmansk silver bowl of 1982 in the New York Museum of Modern Art's collection, and the Tekne 3 electric typewriter of 1964 – although, in this case, a version modified by George Nelson, who softened its hard, architectural lines to make the typewriter more acceptable to the American market. But then, I do remember accompanying Sottsass on a tour of English art colleges in the 1970s when no one knew who he was. Only after students talked about his lectures did the staff realised that they had missed listening to one of the world's greatest designers.

The book's publication follows the exhibition, 'Sottsass, Designer' held at the Los Angeles County Museum earlier this year, which, apparently, is the first time Sottsass has been given a one-man show in America. The book begins with an introduction by Penny Sparke, who sets the scene by placing Sottsass in the Italian Rationalist tradition of the 1920s and 1930s (he began designing in 1946), which rejected the mechanistic approach to design of the Modernists in favour of the more optimistic and humanistic approach that certainly distinguishes his work.

Sparke then introduces the reader to Sottsass's early paintings (although there is no mention of the Yugoslav action painter, Spazzapan), to his early graphics, exhibition design and ceramics with references to Josef Hoffman, Japanese design, Jackson Pollock and Pop Art, and to Sottsass's role as chief consultant designer to Olivetti that led to his work on Olivetti's first computers (one of which won a Compasso d'Oro) and the GE115 already mentioned. These were accompanied by the first electric typewriters, the red-cased Valentine portable manual typewriter (whose attempt to be for typewriters what the Biro was to the fountain pen was ruined by the rising price of oil – and hence of plastics – which is never made clear), teleprinters and office furniture systems.

What is also not made clear is the unique position given by Adriano Olivetti to Sottsass, whose office was underwritten by the company and who was allowed to work for others, provided they were not in competition with Olivetti itself. This enabled Sottsass to design furniture for Poltronova and ceramics for Bitossi - and, because Sottsass was directly answerable to Olivetti's board, to design products for Olivetti that its salespeople did not like. The Tekne 3 was an example of this. Its form was very different to the sculptural shape given by Eliot Noyes to IBM's first golf ball typewriter.

Sparke's introduction also deals with Sottsass's travels to India, Nepal and Burma, his connections with the beat generation in America and Italian radicals such as Superstudio in Italy, arguing that his work with Alchymia in 1979 and his formation of Memphis in 1981 was, in fact, a continuation of his earlier radical designs seen in, for example, the Superboxes of 1968 (inspired by the Beat generation) and the Grey Furniture of 1970 with its Art Deco overtones. Sottsass, Sparke says, believed that the ideals of Modernism could be extended; Mendini, founder of Alchymia, did not.

The furniture, light fittings, silverware, ceramics, textiles and graphics produced by Alchymia and Memphis in the 1980s were notable for their use of both expensive materials like marble, and inexpensive materials like plastics, and plastic laminates in a way that brought to an end the idea that design progressed in a linear fashion. Sottsass's use of materials and colour is discussed by Dennis P Doordan who says that, while Michelangelo liberated form from materials and Frank Lloyd Wright understood the nature of materials, Sottsass explores both materials and colour unfettered by convention or tradition. Hence, in his use of terra cotta, he values the material for its history, and in his celebration of plastic laminates he gives recognition to a material whose use in 1950s Milanese coffee bars and American diners has been ignored by the design profession. For Sottsass, materials are conveyors of sensation − a belief Sottsass Associati developed in the interiors designed for Esprit showrooms in Germany, Austria and Switzerland that were given dramatic colours which broke up a sense of orientation, direction and relationships. Visitors to the stores were expected to navigate their way through a sensorial labyrinth.

The establishment of Sottsass Associati in 1980 not only meant a return to interior design, which had occupied Sottsass in the 1950s and 1960s, but also to architecture, which Sottsass did with his father immediately after the

Second World War, when he worked on projects funded by Marshall Aid. He abandoned architecture because (though the book does not tell you this) once the architect had completed his plans, he lost control of the building. So, one of the real values of the book is that it contains chapters on Sottsass' architecture since the 1980s, and especially on his houses as far afield as the USA, Singapore, Italy and Belgium which are analysed by James Steele. While Sottsass himself acknowledges the influence of Gropius, Le Corbusier and Aldo Rossi, Steele argues that Sottsass is linked to the Italian Rationalists and the Neo-Rationalists (Rossi) by his use of primal forms and colour to evoke poetic associations. Indeed, one could almost argue that Sottsass plays with the Rudolf Steiner blocks beloved by Frank Lloyd Wright, but develops angularities rather than assembling them in a very disciplined way. Sottsass is also interested in symbols (and regards his houses like big pieces of furniture) and is completely against turning everything into a commodity.

The book also attempts to describe Sottsass himself, Steele reflecting on his melancholic, detached and fatalistic attitudes. Some insight is also given by the interview with Sottsass conducted by Emily Zaiden (who also provides maker biographies and company profiles). In it,

he comes across as a man who is out-of-touch with today – who no longer understands the behaviour of young people whose own technology and culture are foreign to him. This may seem surprising because much of the technology is linked to the early computers to whose magical powers he gave physical form. But then, when I knew him well in the 1970s, Sottsass filled his office with young people because, he said, he was finding it difficult to see into the future.

Besides giving a comprehensive overview of Sottsass's work (although there is nothing on his photography, let alone his wonderful writings), the book is lavishly and beautifully illustrated. **RC**

Richard Carr is the author of *Catching up with Sottsass*. Glasgow: The Lighthouse, 1999. ISBN 0953653307

Turner Prize 2006

Tate Britain, London

3 October 2006–14 January 2007

T his year's jury seem to have spread their bets: with a painter, a sculptor, an installation artist and a video artist in the running, there's something for everyone. There's even a whiff of scandal in Turner judge Lynn Barber's candid admission in The Observer that 'none of the judges had seen all the shows'[1] from which they had to pick the shortlist.

The role of the media in disseminating such information is obliquely addressed in Mark Titchner's 'Ergo Ergot'. A screen displays a headache-inducing flicker of Rorschach ink blots interspersed with dates over the last seven years when, according to the human rights group Liberty, the UK government has passed legislation that threatens civil liberties. The aggravating humming noise that fills the room is supposed to lure one's brain into a trance-like state. Titchner's other installation, 'How to Change Behaviour (Tiny Masters of the World Come Out)', takes another sidelong look at belief systems and authority. A huge poster declaims 'Tiny Masters of the World Come Out!'

in the manner of Titchner's previous work commissioned by Platform for Art for Gloucester Road tube station. Set alongside this is a set of rickety apparatus, including what looks like a cross between a wooden pulpit and a teleportation device. Electrical cables and crystals proliferate, as well as hand-carved slogans ('out of darkness into light', 'we take up the task eternal') taken from trades union banners. Titchner's bricolage recombines found texts with elements of fringe spiritual and new-age belief systems, and although he might present these ideas 'without mockery or cynicism',[2] as the catalogue claims, I found the effect rather underwhelming.

Rebecca Warren's vitrines also juxtapose found objects, but in a much more powerful and poetic manner. These roughly made boxes share the deliberately thrown-together aesthetic of the rest of her sculptural practice, and contain discarded lumps of clay, odd hairs, scraps of card and sawdust. Warren situates her work in an artistic and sculptural tradition, creating a dialogue with (male) forebears such as Degas

□ 1. Tomma Abts. *Mino,* 2005. Acrylic and oil on canvas, 48 x 38 cm. Jill and Peter Kraus © the artist

☐ 1

2

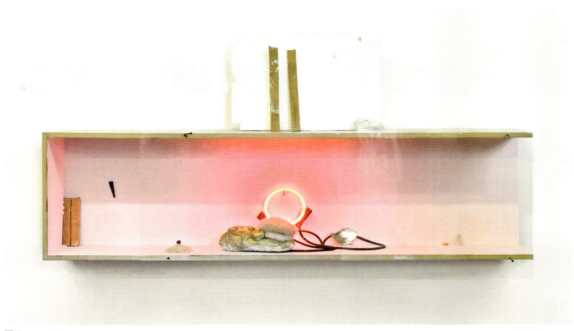

□ 3

□ 2. Phil Collins. *The return of the real/gercegin geri donusu,* 2005. Installation view. Erreala denaren itzulera/el retorno de lo real, sala rekalde, Bilbao, 2006. Courtesy the artist

□ 3. Rebecca Warren. *2001, 2002, 2003, 2004 or 2005,* 2006. Mixed media. 28.6 x 137.8 x 42.5. Courtesy Maureen Paley, London © The artist

□ 4. Rebecca Warren. *Pauline,* 2006. Bronze. Approx 125 x 38 x 41. Courtesy Gordon Watson, London and Maureen Paley, London

□ 4

6

5

☐ 7

and Rodin, and an unmentioned influence for this vitrine series must surely be Beuys. In an interview with Carl Freedman, Warren has stated she is 'interested in the way something can be perceived as having a ritual or religious value'[3] and, indeed, her carefully placed twigs, pompoms, cherry stones and other detritus suggest a ritual drama, lit by small bent tubes of coloured neon.

Also on show are some new works in clay, which, in a move away from her earlier overly sexualised female forms, are squat pieces not modelled on the human body. Closer inspection reveals the same dynamic, rough technique and protruding body parts though. Warren is also exhibiting five pieces in bronze, cast from clay originals and then modified and re-cast. These return to her explorations of female form,

extrapolating from Degas's 'Little Dancer Aged Fourteen' (1880–81). An engagement with bronze as material is evident: in places the rubber from the mould has been left stuck to the sculptures, and in other places Warren has covered the bronze in paint.

In a short film shown at the end of the exhibition, Warren talks about trying to allow the work to define itself, and her methods for achieving this seem to include working and revising her malleable material at speed. The painter Tomma Abts appears to have the same goal, but reaches it by a very different route. She has given all 11 paintings in her exhibition personal names as titles, an indication of how she wishes each finished piece to have its own emotional charge, even personality. The painting as person might be a fruitful analogy, given Abts's technique, which involves laying down a ground of bright acrylic colours (genetic make-up) and then covering or revealing them with smooth layers of oil paints (life experiences). The paintings themselves are formally controlled and resolutely abstract, with the lines of their earlier incarnations visible under the final colour planes. The catalogue quotes Abts as calling the pictures 'a concentrate of the many paintings underneath',[4] and these hidden depths are what give her small canvases such power.

Abts's restraint contrasts with the monumental video piece that represents Phil Collins's work. He is showing 'The return of the real/gercegin geri donusu', a piece originally commissioned for the Istanbul Biennial in 2005. He continued his explorations of contemporary culture's fraught love affair with reality TV by employing the director of a Turkish makeover show to interview 15 Turkish volunteers, all of whom had appeared on TV shows. In a darkened room, the head shots of the director and interviewee are projected onto opposite walls, as if they are facing each other. Prompted by the director, the interviewees retell the stories of their often harrowing lives for a full hour, digressing and repeating themselves. As a viewer, one gets drawn into the drama, almost

forgetting that their stories have become a form of entertainment again. Collins's other move has been to transpose his production company's office to the Tate for the duration of the exhibition, so that visitors can watch his team go about their days of research and phone calls. It seems that Collins's interest lies in exposing the invisible contexts of television: the stories that were not fully told in a few minutes on air, or the months of background work that go in to a show. **JW**

References
1. Barber L. 'How I suffered for art's sake'. *The Observer,* 1 October 2006.
2. Boase G. Mark Titchner. In: Boase G, Carey-Thomas L, Stout K. *Turner Prize 2006.* London: Tate Publishing, 2006.
3. Freedman C. Interview. In: Ruf B (ed). *Rebecca Warren.* Zurich: JRP Ringier, 2005: 24.
4. Carey-Thomas L. Tomma Abts. In: Boase G, Carey-Thomas L, Stout K. *Turner Prize 2006.* London: Tate Publishing, 2006.

□ 8

The RIBA Stirling Prize for Architecture 2006

This month, the architect, Richard Rogers, has attained a summit point in his career in winning the UK RIBA Stirling Prize. The building that has won the prize is not even in Britain, but the architect very much is.

The script for this career could never have been anticipated. One of the most interesting aspects is that early on in their careers, Rogers was in partnership with the equally successful architect, Norman Foster. On the face of it, no two architects could have come from a more different background. Foster, two years younger, comes from a working class background, forged through hard graft in Manchester. Before turning to architecture, he served two years' national service in the Royal Air Force. Rogers' cousin was the famous Italian architect Ernesto Rogers of Milan. After his own military service, Rogers, unlike Foster, might have been called unemployable at 20. He, therefore, took a foundation course at Epsom College of Art, where he had been advised to go by Ernesto Rogers, to get into the Architectural Association School of Architecture. Here, the staff were by no means unanimous about Rogers' actual aptitude for architecture. But he persevered, even though his abysmal drawing skills still handicapped him. After some years, and Rogers' basic qualification (Foster was already getting there, although two years younger), the future opened up. The two sparring partners had met at Yale, where both attended postgraduate architectural courses. Despite some delay, both had learnt to work with each other, and on return to Britain, it was natural that they should form a partnership.

Today, it is interesting to measure the progress and the separate trajectories followed by each individual that led to the neighbouring pinnacles attained by the two practices. Both are of comparable reputation, but very different in output. Rogers' practice is the smaller of the two, but both employ significant numbers. There are different methodologies, however. Ken Shuttleworth (who claims to have designed the famous 'Gherkin' building in the City of London for the practice) left suddenly after its launch. In Rogers' practice the equivalent anchorman has been Mike Davies. In output there is very considerable overlap between each practice. This is best revealed through airport design using the principle of the 'big shed'. The basic airport prototype, it has to be admitted, was Stansted, by Foster. Terminal 5 at Heathrow, where gigantic 'tree' columns are a

□ 1. Outside *Barajas Airport Terminal,* Madrid. Photo credit: Katsuhisa Kida

□ 2. Escalators at *Barajas Airport Terminal,* Madrid. Photo credit: Manuel Renau

□ 1

□ 2

□ 3

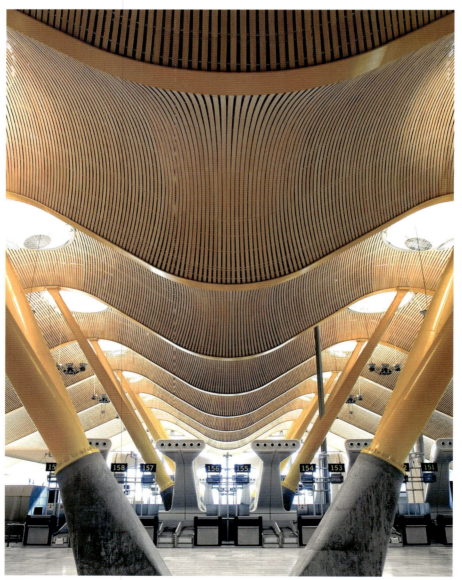

□ 4

development of the much-praised Stansted. Therefore, Madrid, with its long 1.25 km plan is the amplification of this formula.

Once the technology of the support structure and the span has been provided (as at Stansted) it has simply been a question of larger and longer. Where Madrid has differed from Stansted is the generous (and also informative) application of colour, as well as of a timber inner lining and cladding. Rogers has increasingly resorted to the use of timber in this way. The Welsh National Assembly building was also entered by the Rogers practice and, again, displayed the imaginative use of timber as a core cladding, like a sweeping, large-trunked oak tree. But this project has been outclassed by the Madrid entry.

Rogers has not always got it right, whereas one could say that even with such a large practice, Foster seldom gets it wrong, and even the Millennium Bridge fiasco was quickly rectified by the engineers, as was their task. Rogers' Dome for London is simply not a success, and squats at Greenwich, political bait for possible casino implantation. Rogers' new Law Courts for Bordeaux look more like a winery, (or perish the thought – a distillery) with the vat-like truncations that serve light to the seven courts of justice. Invited to the World Trade Centre site to design a fourth tower for the complex, Rogers' practice seeks to offer transparency in the best glazing mode of today. The iconic symbolism of the material is undoubtedly appropriate, when the glass facades all rise beyond the roofline together with heavy (reassuring) steel cross-bracing,

designed to provide full support for the tower in the contingency of a new attack. Psychologically reassuring – but then David Childs of SOM architects has heavily strengthened his own final tower designs. This is the architecture of defence in the 'war against terror' ...

Throughout his career, Rogers has shown great dexterity in always meeting his clients' wishes, and persuading them of his social vision. This ran from the Pompidou Centre, through the Lloyds Building in the City of London and The European Court of Human Rights. Rogers, the individual, continues to embrace major environmental causes and the practice itself is still established on the basis of a salary structure where the most junior employees' wages are related to the salaries of senior staff, who might otherwise, as in the corporate world, go ballistic. **Editor**

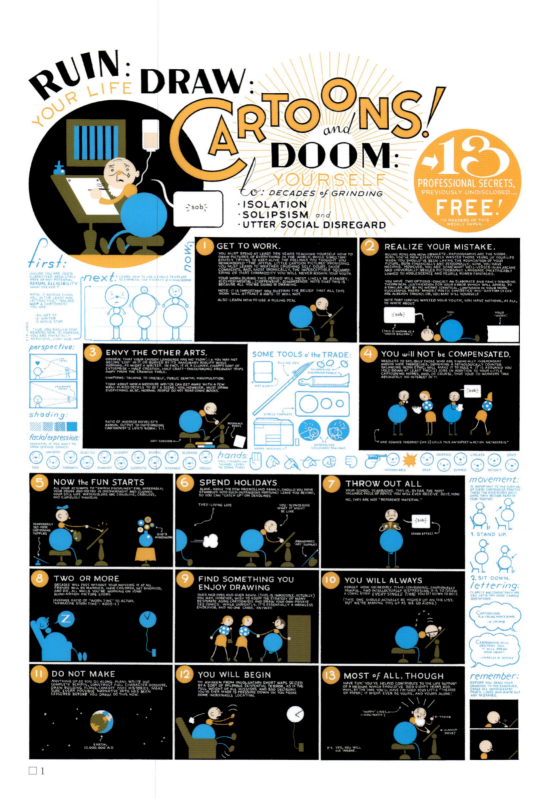

☐ 1. Chris Ware. *Draw Cartoons—Ruin Your Life,* 2003. Pen and ink with coloured pencil and gouache. Collection of the artist. Reproduced with permission of the artist

Unmasking the heroes of American comic art

Masters of American Comics

The Newark Museum, New Jersey

15 September 2006–28 January 2007

The contemporary comic genre contains many novel and sophisticated artistic expressions. Art Spiegelman's Pulitzer Prize-winning *MAUS* and Neil Gaiman's *The Sandman*, winner of the 1991 World Fantasy Award for short fiction, could be called fine art storytelling.[1] And the comics drawn by Chris Ware in his Acme Novelty Library would find a comfortable home among fine art books. Reproduced in gilt and embossed bindings reminiscent of old and rare books, Ware's work is at once classic and modern, recalling Winsor McCay's beautifully designed and coloured layouts. In the works of these and other contemporary masters of comic art are signs pointing to a venerable lineage.

While, today, the comic genre in the US has been marginalised to specialist audiences and subgenres, its overall appeal continues to grow with every new transformation, including the astounding commercial success of anime (Japanese cartoons) and manga (Japanese comic books), and the American versions of them. The more recent incarnations are merely additional evidence of the flexibility and relevance of the best comics and graphic novels.

In fact, for more than 100 years, many notable artists have contributed to a visual vocabulary that builds on tradition and is also culturally specific.

Now on view in New York and Newark, New Jersey, 'Masters of American Comics' began as a joint venture between the Armand Hammer Museum of Art and Cultural Center, University of California at Los Angeles, and the Museum of Contemporary Art, Los Angeles (20 November 2005–12 March 2006). The exhibit travelled to the Milwaukee Art Museum (27 April–20 August 2006) before opening, in two parts, at the Jewish Museum in New York City and the Newark Museum (15 September 2006–28 January 2007). A large-format, full-colour catalogue contains an introductory essay by independent writer and curator John Carlin, who curated the Whitney's 1983 'Comic Art Show', and contributions from, among others, columnist Pete Hamill, comic artists Jules Feiffer and Matt Groening, and authors Dave Eggers and Jonathan Safran Foer.[2]

The show and catalogue tell a story of tradition and innovation, of ground-breakers and the artists of the future who, as children, grew up devouring strips, comic books and, later, graphic novels; who drew picture stories in their rooms, in the margins of their school books and in their self-made publications, dreaming of following in the footsteps of such pioneers as McCay (*Little Nemo in Slumberland*), Will Eisner (*The Spirit*), George Herriman (*Krazy Kat*), Jack Kirby (*Captain America*), Charles M Schultz (*Peanuts*) and Harvey Kurtzman (*MAD magazine*). Together, the masters of American comics have rendered comedies, tragedies, parodies of human folly and psychologically complex explorations of culture and the self. From the frames and panels of the earliest comics to the more complex layouts that evolved over time, a complete range of treatments and subjects have been offered to avid readers. In fact, the graphic language of each comic can be considered singular and of interest in itself, aside from any specific characters or storylines.

Originally, Spiegelman proposed the exhibit; it took years to bring together the more than 900 drawings, newspaper pages, graphic novels and comic books on view. To accommodate this vast material, the Jewish Museum's exhibit focuses on 14 comic artists chronologically: Eisner, Kirby, Kurtzman, R. Crumb (*Zap* comics; *Fritz the Cat*), Gary Panter (Slash and Raw magazines) and Ware (*Jimmy Corrigan: The Smartest Kid on Earth*). The artists shown at the Newark Museum provide a history of comic strips in the early 20th century: McCay, Lyonel Feininger (*Kin-der-Kids*; *Wee Willie Winkie's World*), Herriman, EC Segar (*Thimble Theatre*, *Popeye*), Frank King (*Gasoline Alley*), Chester Gould (*Dick Tracy*), Milton Caniff (*Terry and the Pirates*, *Steve Canyon*) and Schultz.

Although some commentators have drawn comparisons between early cave paintings and comics, a more direct line can be traced to English artist William Hogarth's A Harlot's Progress (1732) and then through the great 19th-century British caricaturists (Thomas Rowlandson, James Gillray), with side trips to Europe – for example, the satires of Rudolphe Topffer in Switzerland and Wilhelm Busch in Germany.[3] In America, Thomas Nast (1840–1902) developed a complex graphic style with his signature cross-hatching that influenced many later American cartoonists. But these and other connections do not explain the enormous growth and popularity of comics in 20th-century America. The answer can be found in culturally specific conditions and changes that opened the door for skilled draftsmen to find work and express their vision to a large audience through mass-produced periodicals. Comics are art for the masses, a form of storytelling that harkens back to folk traditions – a type of magic realism filled with drama, offbeat characters and fantastic storylines but rooted in human fears, hopes and dreams. Comics became a contemporary form of

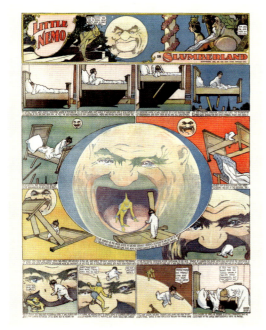

2

3

4

5

□ 9

□ 11

□ 10

American Comics', a sideline exhibit of more than 70 works on view at the Jewish Museum during the main exhibit's run. 'Superheroes' is guest curated by Jerry Robinson, who began working with Batman's creators in 1939. Robinson is credited with developing the character of the Joker, as well as naming Robin, the boy wonder. Fifteen comic artists and writers are featured, all of Jewish background. Artists include Joe Shuster and Jerry Siegel (Superman); Bob Kane and Bill Finger (Batman); Kirby (Captain America, The X-Men, Fantastic Four); and Mort Meskin (Johnny Quick, Vigilante).

After viewing either part of the exhibit, visitors who hadn't planned to travel to the other part may want to alter their plans, for without the other half the story is incomplete. And a third part of the puzzle – the place of women in the history of American comic art – is left untold. Fortunately, two exhibits concurrently open in New York redress the balance: 'She Draws Comics: 100 Years of America's Women Cartoonists' at the Museum of Contemporary Comic Art (MoCCA) in Soho, showcasing work by women comic and cartoon artists over the span of a century,[4] and 'Telling Tales: Contemporary Women Cartoonists' at the Adam Baumgold Gallery on New York's upper East Side, focusing on artists working during the past four decades.[5] And in November, the Jewish Museum will host a panel discussion of women comic artists.[6]

This absence is glaring when one realises that there have, indeed, been women artists and protagonists throughout comic art history. Nell Brinkley was a turn-of-the-century feminist cartoonist; Dale Messick, the first nationally syndicated woman comic artist, debuted her Brenda Starr: Reporter in 1940 in the Sunday comics; and Wonder Woman first appeared in 1941 in *All Star* Comics #8. The appearance of women on the comic scene is notable, particularly, from the mid-sixties on, when the growing underground movement attracted even more women to the field as a means to express their perspectives.

Just as the curators of 'Superheroes' have highlighted the Jewish backgrounds of the artists shown, connecting their marginalised status to superhero themes, Robbins and Nadel have brought together artists and work that reveal the egalitarian and subversive potential of the comic format. Other examples of those who have draw comics to offer an alternate to prevailing views are Kurtzman's wartime works, which brought out the darker side of loss rather than the glory of war; Crumb's story of down-and-out black delta blues man, Charlie Patton; and Spiegelman's personal account of the Holocaust in *MAUS*. Teens and young adults today spend a considerable amount of money on graphic novels and manga that express their sense of alienation with irony and wit.

Grasping the full extent of comic art in America would take years of reading and enjoying the comics themselves. 'Masters of American Comics' functions more as an introduction than a comprehensive survey. Fortunately, the exhibit catalogue fills in most of the gaps. A lavish homage to the artists and their work, the book deserves a place on the shelves of longtime fans of comic art and those who want to discover the surprises to be found within these miniature theaters. **CDM**

Footnotes

1 MAUS first appeared in *Raw* magazine from 1980–91 and, later, was collected into volumes. In it, Spiegelman (American; b. 1948, Stockholm) jolted readers into new insights on the Holocaust by stripping down and then amplifying a subject that has lost some sting due to superficial and uneven treatments. In Gaiman's series of graphic novels illustrated by Dave McKean, the World War II-era DC comics character the Sandman, a Batman-esque superhero, is a darker figure who rules over the realm of Dreaming.
2. Masters of American Comics, edited by John Carlin, Paul Karasik and Brian Walker (New Haven and London: Hammer Museum and the Museum of Contemporary Art, Los Angeles, in association with Yale University Press, 2005).
3. Topffer published *The Adventures of Obadiah Oldbuck* in 1837, now considered the earliest comic book. In 1842, *The Adventures of Obadiah Oldbuck* became the first comic book published in the U S Poet and artist Busch began publishing caricatures in 1859. In 1865, *Max and Moritz (A Story of Seven Boyish Pranks)*, for which he is best known, appeared.
4. 'She Draws Comics: 100 Years of America's Women Cartoonists' opened at MoCCA on 20 May 2006 and closes on 6 November. The show is curated by comic artist, author and women's historian Trina Robbins, a key contributor to the early underground zine movement in the seventies. More than one hundred works by approximately fifty artists – including Nell Brinkley; Dale Messick. Sara Varon and Jessica Abel – are on view.
5. 'Telling Tales: Contemporary Women Cartoonists' opened at the Adam Baumgold Gallery on 5 September 2006 and closed on 14 October. The show included cartoons by Roz Chast, Debbie Drechsler and Lauren Weinstein.
6. Other related programmes offered by the Jewish Museum include a panel discussion of the golden age of comics; a screening of the film 'Comic Book Confidential'; and appearances by Chris Ware at the museum, and Matt Groening, creator of 'The Simpsons', and Gary Panter (the 'King of Punk Art') at the 92nd Street YMCA.

□ 1

□ 1. Wassily Kandinsky. *Improvisation 30 (Cannons),*
1913, The Art Institute of Chicago

□ 2. Wassily Kandinsky. *Improvisation 2 (Funeral
March),* 1908. Moderna Museet, Stockholm

□ 2

Kandinsky: The Path to Abstraction

Tate Modern, London

22 June–1 October 2006

Kunstmuseum, Basel

21 October 2006–4 February 2007

For decades, art history taught us that Kandinsky was the greatest pioneer of abstract art, the artist who removed the subject matter from painting. The great ideological debate between abstraction and figuration has given way to a more considered view of the dialogue between the two, yet many misguided views and myths remain.

Paul Overy's study of Kandinsky remains the most satisfying. 'Kandinsky's approach to abstraction was supported by constant thought and examination of the problems involved and his theoretical statements often anticipate the paintings. Certainly, he was by far and away the most important artist to experiment with abstraction around 1910 and the only one who developed a thoroughly coherent style.'[1] Norbert Lynton shares Overy's frustration with the preoccupation by scholars with abstraction at the expense of an adequate appraisal of Kandinsky's work. Referring to the Tate exhibition this summer, and the accompanying catalogue and wall text, he states:

> We read in two places that Kandinsky was 'a pioneer in the development of a new visual language – abstraction', but all art is 'abstraction', even a Constable landscape. No one tackles the question of what is meant by the term here. The path is pointed to, again and again, and the exhibits are produced in evidence of his progress along it, but its goal is left vague.[2]

Russian-born Wassily Kandinsky was a prolific and inspiring artist and intellectual, whose writings were a key to understanding abstraction as the expression of 'inner necessity' on the part of the artist, whose messianic vision would lead society to a better world. By limiting the study of Kandinsky to the emergence of abstraction, this reduces the value of his work, which is full of invention and originality. His extraordinary blend of apocalypse and neo-Platonic vision was the product of the tense period during the first two decades of the 20th century. The influence of the theosophical ideas of Madame Blavatsky and the anthroposophy of Rudolph Steiner on Kandinsky's writings of the pre-1914 period have been overstated by certain historians, and latterly journalists, and used to undermine Kandinsky's importance as a painter.

Kandinsky's theoretical works have, during the last few years, become the hunting ground of art historians and scholars. (His paintings have been relatively neglected by critics and the view that Kandinsky was more important as a historical phenomenon and a theorist is still widely held.) These scholars have taken an especial delight in pointing out the 19th-century sources from which many of Kandinsky's theoretical writings derive and seem never to have cast more than a second glance at the paintings which they help to illuminate.[3]

In spite of the glorious manifestation of colour in Kandinsky's paintings, foreboding characterises many of his works:

> The sense of impending disintegration and chaos that his paintings of this year communicate show that Kandinsky was fully aware of the imminent collapse of the pre-war 1914 world. It was not only an international but also a personal crisis. A lesser artist would probably not have survived this; his

*paintings after the war would have been
hollow echoes of his earlier style. Perhaps
because he was a mature man in his late 40s
who had only taken up painting after an
exacting intellectual academic training,
Kandinsky was able to survive as an artist
and to develop a style, an artistic language,
which enabled him to come to terms with the
post-war world. Kandinsky's later, geometric
works shocked many of his former admirers
in Germany so deeply that they broke off
relations with him. Even today many critics
still prefer the Munich paintings. But his later
work was, in fact, a perfectly coherent and
necessary development, which enabled
Kandinsky during the Bauhaus period at
least to match the quality of his finest Munich
works and during his final years in Paris to
excel them in power and range.[4]*

The relationship between art and music is
central to an examination of Kandinsky's work
in the exhibition this summer at Tate Modern,
with paintings entitled 'Composition' and
'Improvisation'. Kandinsky also wrote and
published poetry in which he emphasised the
sound of words, rather than their meaning. The
works themselves are among the outstanding
masterpieces of the 20th century. His life and
work are those of a brilliant and prolific
intellectual artist; as the exhibition testified, his
works have a pivotal position and enduring
quality that was recognised by artist
contemporaries of Kandinsky, better perhaps
than subsequent commentators and art
historians. Diego Rivera, in 1931, on the occasion
of an exhibition in San Francisco, stated:

*I know of nothing more real than the
painting of Kandinsky – nor anything more
true and nothing more beautiful. A painting
by Kandinsky gives no image of earthly life
– it is life itself. If one painter deserves the
name 'creator', it is he. He organises matter
as matter was organised, otherwise the
Universe would not exist. He opened a
window to look inside the All. Someday,
Kandinsky will be the best known and best
loved of men.[5]*

'Kandinsky: The Path to Abstraction' was
claimed to be the first major exhibition in
Britain to focus on the paintings of Wassily
Kandinsky (1866–1944). It was met with a mix
of praise and hostility, ridicule of theosophy and
a simplified reliance on the theory of
synthanaesia, the ability to see music.[6] In 1999,
however, the Royal Academy showed some 140
Kandinskys from every period – all small-scale
works on paper and cardboard. The Tate
exhibition represents a precise period in
Kandinsky's career, 1905–21, one that includes
the necessary elements of his development
without attempting to appraise the complex
issues pertaining to Kandinsky's vast *oeuvre*.
The exhibition examines the most popular
period in Kandinsky's career spanning his time
in Munich and Murnau in the second decade of
the 20th century, his return to Moscow in 1914
and his departure there in 1922 for Weimar via
Berlin, where he accepted a teaching post at the
Bauhaus. In those 13 years, the spiritual, social
and political circumstances of the world had
been shattered. Kandinsky's friends and fellow
artists, Franz Marc and August Macke, were

□ 3

□ 3. Wassily Kandinsky. *Murnau with Church II,* 1910.
Collection Van Abbe Museum, Eindhoven

□ 4. Wassily Kandinsky. *Improvisation 35,* 1914,
Kunstmuseum Basel

□ 5. Wassily Kandinsky, *Cossacks,* 1910–11, Tate, London

□ 4

□ 5

among the millions of young men slaughtered in the First World War.

The old boundaries and balances of power of pre-1914 Europe had been swept away. Germany had been defeated and humiliated. Russia had gone through the pain and hope of revolution and, already, disillusion was beginning to set in. The war caused a traumatic break in the intellectual and artistic life of Europe. Artists and writers had been in revolt against the sterile, complacent pre-1914 society with its obsolete values. And that society had been swept away in a more devastating and terrible way than they could ever have dreamed of.[7]

Wassily Kandinsky was born in Moscow in 1866, the son of a wealthy Siberian tea merchant and his wife, Lydia Ivanovna Tiheeva, from Moscow. In 1871, the family moved to Odessa, where Wassily stayed on with his mother after his parents divorce. He learnt cello

and piano from a young age and attended a humanistic secondary school there. In 1885, Kandinsky moved back to Moscow where he attended the University of Moscow to study law and economics. After qualifying, he travelled to Vologda where he published two articles on peasant law and paganism among Siberian tribes. He painted and he discovered peasant folk art. Following the legal and ground roots experience in Russia, he made two important trips to Paris. In 1893, Kandinsky completed his PhD on the legality of labourer's wages. He was also offered a position in the Faculty of Law, University of Moscow.

In 1895, Kandinsky saw the 'Haystack' series of paintings by Claude Monet, on show in Moscow. He also had what has been recognised as that of a synaesthetic experience while listening to Wagner. He later wrote: 'I saw all my colours in spirit, before my eyes. Wild, almost mad lines drew themselves in front of me'. Now financially independent, he moved to Munich in 1896 and enrolled in art classes. As a student there he met Alexei Jawlensky, Marianne von Werefkin and Paul Klee. By 1901, Kandinsky was also writing art reviews, particularly for Sergei Diaghilev's Moscow progressive art journal Mir Iskusstva. Kandinsky's paintings in gouache, temperas and small works in oil were mostly landscapes with legends and scenes from mediaeval Russian art. He had his first exhibition in Germany the same year, and travelled back to Russia. He met Gabriele Münter, with whom he lived for ten years, and was actively involved with artists, teaching and exhibitions. Greatly inspired again by his Russian heritage on a journey back to Moscow via Venice and Vienna, he wrote to Münter: 'I have a very strange sensation here in Moscow. Hundreds of memories, partly forgotten pictures, the whole character of the genuine Russian town which I feel and understand even today, these churches, carriages, flats people who are so distant yet so familiar. I have been away from her for seven years and only now, for the first time, I am having these sensations'. Kandinsky created and published a small book, a series of woodcuts, 'Poems without Words', inspired by Russian folk picture books. He also worked on embroidery, jewellery, clothes and furniture.

Central to his career as a theorist, Kandinsky began to investigate 'form' in art – form created from inner necessity. Kandinsky travelled extensively in Italy and to Paris with Gabriele Münter. He had his first solo exhibition in Munich in 1905, and painted, exhibited and wrote extensively. It was not until 1908 when Kandinsky was 42 that he began to produce major works. He also worked on his art theory, in particular, Concerning the Spiritual in Art, which was published in 1911.

Kandinsky and Franz Marc formed a group, Die Blaue Reiter (The Blue Rider), which, with Die Brücke (The Bridge) was the most important organisation of artists in pre-1914 Germany. Its first exhibition included artists from outside of Germany: Robert Delaunay and Douanier (Henri) Rousseau. The second exhibition included a formidable range of work by Arp, Braque, Derain, Goncharova, Heckel, Kirkner, Klee, Larionov, Malevich, Nolde, Pechstein, Picasso and Vlaminck. Kandinsky, Marc and Macke produced The Blaue Reiter Almanac, which included articles on music, theatre and art. Kandinsky wrote half of the articles and translated articles from Russian. The work included children's art and folk art, for Kandinsky was interested in 'the organic interior roots of art in general', as much as the finished work. The interaction between art and the life of human society was essential, as was Kandinsky's Russian Orthodox Christian faith. According to Paul Overy, Kandinsky's faith is a fact rarely considered by critics of his work.[8]

In 'Reminiscences' Kandinsky draws many parallels between art and Christianity. He compares art to religion in that its development does not consist of new discoveries that controvert former theories (as in science) but of new truths, which grow organically from the old, but do not render the old truths obsolete.[9]

Kandinsky remained optimistic about the

☐ 6

future even when war destroyed so much of society. He equated representational painting with traditionalism. When he published a revised version of his autobiographical essay in 1918 he cut out many references to Christianity, out of the necessary respect for the Communist regime, even though he was never a Communist himself. If they were published, today, they would no doubt be dismissed along with references to theosophy and Steiner and further spiritual views that have been unpopular in mainstream visual arts for most of the 20th century. The path to abstraction is undeniably vital to placing Kandinsky in a historical context and in the wider scheme of art history. In the process, one hopes that the essential meaning of Kandinsky's work will be clarified and linked to issues in contemporary art practices. Although he had strong ideological links with individuals, groups and institutions, Kandinsky has to be viewed as a unique, and rare talent whose extraordinary faith in art, ideas, spirituality, Christian redemption produced paintings that are in Rivera's words, 'life itself'. Kandinsky's paintings convey life in its intensity and complexity. He expresses drama, destruction, complex relationships, candid beauty, courage and redemption through exquisite orchestrations of colour and line, like no other artist before or since. **JMcK**

References
1. Overy P. *Kandinsky: The Language of the Eye*. London: Elek, 1969: 13.
2. Lynton N. 'The infectious impurity of Kandinsky's "visual music": abstraction's true colours'. *Times Literary Supplement*, 21 July 2006: 18.
3. Overy P. *Op cit*: 31.
4. *Ibid*: 17.
5. *Ibid*: 11.
6. Ward O. 'The man who heard his paintbox hiss'. *Telegraph*, 10 June 2006.
7. *Ibid*: 15.
8. *Ibid*: 19.
9. *Ibid*: 29.

David Hockney Portraits

National Portrait Gallery, London

12 October 2006–21 January 2007

'What an artist is trying to do for people is bring them closer to something, because of course art is about sharing: you wouldn't be an artist unless you wanted to share an experience, a thought.' David Hockney

David Hockney's portraiture has become well known in recent years, with his prodigious output using watercolour on an unprecedented scale and his published work on the subject of optical devices such as the camera lucida. Although portraiture has run through his *oeuvre* since his teenage years, this is the first retrospective devoted to the genre.

'David Hockney Portraits' is the most comprehensive survey of Hockney's portraits ever shown. It features over 150 works, including paintings, drawings, prints, sketchbooks and photo collages, spanning 50 years from 1955 to 2005. 'David Hockney Portraits' opened in Boston and travelled to Los Angeles before coming to London. It is appropriate that it should be shown in England and on the East and West coasts of the USA, for these are the places where Hockney has made his home, and from which his friendships, the subjects of his finest works, have developed.

The distinctive optimism, the saturated palette, the varied and life-affirming oeuvre, has been absorbed into public consciousness more than most living artists, for Hockney is quite rightly one of the most celebrated artists in Britain today. Yet the familiarity that has come

about through media attention (his paintings reproduce extremely well) does nothing to obscure the element of surprise and the sheer joy at seeing the exhibition at the National Portrait Gallery. The exhibition brings together a great range of Hockney's work in many different media that express personal and heartfelt emotions with a tenderness that it is a privilege to experience. The scale and range of the work, and the level of intimate engagement with the process and the subjects, is prompted by a rare faith and trust in human relations.

In Hockney, we experience what George Steiner in *On Difficulty and Other Essays*[1] identified as a lost quality in contemporary literature - a space afforded around figures. For all the intimacy, Hockney also allows a privacy and respect around his characters. The product is compelling. Although Hockney works in the traditional genres of portraiture, still-life and landscape, he has been innovative at all stages of his career. There is a touching candour and unpretentious quality that personifies his life and work. The exhibition starts with Hockney's very early self-portraits and studies of his father created during his student years at Bradford School of Art. A high point of the exhibition are the marvellous, almost life-size, double portraits of 'Henry Geldzahler and Christopher Scott' (1969), 'American Collectors (Mr and Mrs Weisman)' (1968), 'My Parents' (1977) and the splendid 'Mr and Mrs Clark and Percy' (1970-71), which was first shown at the National

1

Portrait Gallery in 1971. In these works, there is both drama and ambiguity between the sitters, a pivotal quality in Hockney's work. The exhibition is accompanied by a comprehensive, fully illustrated catalogue by curators Sarah Howgate and Barbara Stern Shapiro, with essays by Mark Glazebrook, Marco Livingstone and Edmund White.[2]

In an exhibition such as 'David Hockney Portraits', one is inevitably drawn to biographical details to glean the process of the development of such a prodigious talent. The studies and paintings of Hockney's parents, individually and together provide considerable evidence for Hockney's precocious technical skill and the tenderness of relationships that formed the emotional building blocks for a lifetime of friendships and artistic fruition. The depictions of his mother represent some of the finest images of older age.

David Hockney was the fourth of five children born to Kenneth and Laura Hockney. Both were independent and unconventional individuals. Hockney's father was an accountant with unconventional views and strong politics. He was a conscientious objector during the war, and later was actively opposed to nuclear arms. He influenced his son in a number of ways, not least being his stylish appearance and a penchant for spotted bow ties, a large collection of spectacles and false teeth for different occasions. He introduced his son to the theatre, opera and music. According to Hockney, his father taught him not to care what the neighbours thought. Hockney's mother was a strict vegetarian, a devout Methodist and

teetotaller. An unconventional and highly ethical stance was accompanied by a warm and affectionate upbringing; she was always supportive of his artistic career. Hockney's desire to portray the most candid experience of his sitters is illustrated by the fact that he chose the day of his father's funeral to portray his mother. In doing so, he created an image of unveiled human suffering, a moving and outstanding testament to both of his parents.

Hockney's work is often confrontational in manner, psychologically as well as technically - the forward-tilted portrait of Jonathan Silver looks illness and mortality in the eye. The loss of friends to AIDS in Los Angeles in particular, was devastating; further, it symbolised the end of an emancipated sexuality and freedom and tolerance that had drawn Hockney and many others to LA in the 1960s. The contribution made by Hockney as an artist to the gay liberation movement from the 1960s is examined by Edmund White in his catalogue essay, 'The Lineaments of Desire':

From the very beginning, literature, homosexual desire and tributes to friends came together as sources in David Hockney's work. He would remain true to these three influences until the present. Hockney took up gay subject matter before almost anyone else - and the amazing thing is that he got away with it ... Hockney's cool detachment and our sense that he has other, strictly artistic designs on us direct our attention away from all these smooth, bare buttocks.[3]

Hockney has said of his early works:

What one must remember about some of

☐ 2

these pictures is that they were partly propaganda of something that hadn't been propagandised, especially among students, as a subject: homosexuality. I felt it should be done. Nobody else would use it as a subject because it was part of me; it was a subject I could treat humorously. I loved the line, 'We two boys together clinging'; it's a marvellous, beautiful, poetic line.[4]

A characteristic of Hockney's portraiture is the manner in which he has used the same sitters over many decades. Celia Birtwell has remained one of Hockney's closest friends. She is one of the few women to be painted and drawn by Hockney. He describes her thus:

Celia has a beautiful face, a very rare face with lots of things in it which appeal to me. It shows aspects of her, like her intuitive knowledge and her kindness, which I think is the greatest virtue. To me she's such a special person ... Portraits aren't just made up of drawing, they are made up of other insights as well. Celia is one of the few girls I know really well. I've drawn her so many times and knowing her makes it always slightly different. I don't bother getting the likeness in her face because I know it so well. She has many faces and I think if you looked through all the drawings I've done of her, you'd see that they don't look alike.[5]

Celia Birtwell, who first sat for Hockney in 1969, recently observed:

He's an amusing person. He's got a sense of irony and wit that appears in his work. And he's totally devoted to his art. Nothing comes in the way of David painting. He's no young man anymore, but the energy and passion is *just as strong. It's something that is within him. Never fussy, never cute – just right.*[5]

'David Hockney Portraits' reflects the artist's loyalty to lifelong friends that, when viewed *en masse* in the exhibition, makes a powerfully humanist stance. The portraits of Gregory Evans are a case in point. Evans has remained a close companion, assistant and model for over 30 years. The languid 'Gregory Leaning Nude' is intimate, evoking the tender relationship between artist and subject. He is reminiscent of the noble boys in Botticelli's painting, the archetypal young man of classical literature. The drawings of John Fitzherbert, with whom Hockney has lived in Los Angeles and London for the past decade, are particularly fine. Informal poses while travelling, or going about daily life – sleeping, reading, cooking – exude a tender acceptance of life and self.

In 2002, David Hockney sat for Lucian Freud, whose working method was somewhat different to Hockney's. Freud required Hockney to sit for almost 100 hours. Hockney, on the other hand, took just over a day to complete his portrait of Freud. Using the traditional medium of watercolour, Hockney employs quite a different approach. Watercolour was never intended in the manner in which Hockney now uses it. He writes:

Overcoming the technical difficulties of the watercolour medium for large-scale works was a solvable problem. The main difficulty is that washes have to be put on horizontally, but drawing really has to be done vertically to enable one to see it. As this all developed it opened out the medium, leading eventually to the large double portraits.[6]

Each couple in the double portraits are seated on the same swivel chairs, against the same floorboards. Four sheets of paper are placed together so that the overall size is over a metre high (one large sheet would buckle under the weigh of the moisture in the paint). Watercolour is not, however, an easy medium for portraiture, or on this scale. Where oil paint can be scraped and overpainted, any mark in watercolour cannot properly be removed. Overpainting becomes muddy, the paper support can be damaged. Watercolour is ideally suited to small-scale landscapes - the washes revealing light and suggesting atmosphere. Hockney has chosen watercolour, however, for its fluid, quick application so that the 'double portrait' is captured in a single sitting as opposed to the separate sittings of each individual (traditionally used in a double or group portrait). Hockney's ambition is to capture the relationship between his sitters.

As with his own appearance, Hockney manages in his portraits to co-ordinate and orchestrate shoes, clothing, the arrangement of feet, the placement of hands and the bases of the swivel chairs in an original and flamboyant formal arrangement that is utterly human and aesthetically satisfying. Hockney's love and admiration of his friends as subjects are conveyed to the viewer with a sense of great immediacy – the economy of line, the gorgeous colour – so that when one looks at the splendid portraits of Henry Geldzahler, who loved

☐3

□ 4

flamboyant outfits and posing for Hockney, one wants to know him better. When one reads of his death, and Hockney's recollection, 'I expected him to grow into a marvellous, crotchety old man. I would have enjoyed that', and looks at the drawings of Henry on his deathbed, one experiences a great sense of loss. Hockney imbues his own personal loss with a universal poignancy and great compassion.

Hockney's friend, Marco Livingstone, the subject of several portraits and the author of the essay in the Encounters catalogue[7] wrote 'Sitting for Hockney', in David Hockney: Painting on Paper (2003). In it, he reveals many of the artist's motives and methods:

In every case, no matter what the relationship, Hockney was interested in capturing not just the appearance of the sitters but something of their psychology and their interaction with each other. This, he soon discovered, was most visible from their body language: whether they acknowledged each other's presence from the way they sat or seemed to exist in separate spheres; whether they touched or at least approached each other, or seemed on the other hand to be recoiling; whether they seemed at ease and affectionate or tense and mistrustful.[8]

David Hockney has always been a fine draughtsman and committed to traditional skills in art. For years now, he has campaigned for figurative art. Although he always placed great importance on drawing and painting, he has also been interested in experiments in photography and computer-assisted art. In 1999, Hockney quite amazed the art world with his publication of Secret Knowledge (Thames and Hudson, London). His study revealed that the Old Masters of Western art had often used optical devices. Thames and Hudson have recently (2006) republished this title.

The 'Twelve Portraits After Ingres in a Uniform Style' (1999–2000), shown in the National Gallery's exhibition 'Encounters: New Art from Old' in 2000, consist of 12 portraits of uniformed National Gallery attendants. They were drawn from life in Hockney's London studio between 16 December 1999 and 11 January 2000. As with many recent works, these portraits were drawn in a single session lasting between three and five hours. They are lively, intense and individual.

On his return to Los Angeles, Hockney began to play about with his drawn images, photocopying and enlarging parts of the drawings. Photo collages such as 'My Mother, Bolton Abbey, Yorkshire, Nov 1982' (1982) are remarkable and original images. Seen alongside drawings and etchings, one can link his masterly use of space with the large-scale landscapes and opera sets he did in the USA.

The resulting fractured images, which recall the post-Cubist experiments of his photocollages of the early 1980s exaggerate the imposing physical presence of the figures and call their attention to the way that their personality and identity are conveyed as much through their manual gestures as through their physiognomy and facial expression. Created with the assistance of a photo-mechanical process, these 'copies' also bring full circle the dialogue with lenses and optical instruments that lay behind the creation of the original drawings themselves, for which he had availed himself of a camera lucida.[9]

In the late 1970s, Hockney became intensely interested in the work of Ingres - especially in his technique - believing that Ingres might have used an optical device known as a camera lucida, patented in 1807. It was, Hockney believed, used to create a quick likeness of a sitter unknown to the artist. It is 'essentially nothing more than a small prism (mounted at the end of a metal arm) through which the subject is refracted and reconstituted as a virtual image on a sheet of paper'.[10]

Hockney corresponded with a number of people on the subject, including art historian Professor Martin Kemp (University of Oxford), whose book The Science of Art: Optical Themes in Western Art from Brunelleschi to Seurat (London, 1990) was of great interest to Hockney, who drew Kemp's portrait with a camera lucida on 22 June 1999. Speaking of Hockney, Kemp recalls his first meeting:

All artists are intelligent, but not all are intelligent in that articulate way. He had extraordinary curiosity. Not long after that, I sat for him. He was doing a series of camera lucida drawings. He used the camera, for no more than two minutes, as a basic mapping device of the facial features as they were at a particular moment. All the rest is then 'eyeballed', as he called it – directly looking at someone. He was sitting very close to me. It's a kind of mental striptease because nobody ever looks at you that hard. That ferocity of scrutiny – of your nose and your eyes or whatever – is wonderfully disconcerting, to have two eyes tick-tocking from the paper to you with searing concentration.[11]

By the time Hockney returned to London in December 1999 to work on the National Gallery portraits, he had produced some 280 drawings with the same device. Hockney then wrote his radical and controversial Secret Knowledge to consolidate his research into the use of optical devices and lenses used by artists from the Renaissance to the 19th century. As Livingstone points out, the camera lucida enabled Hockney to learn a great deal about the topography of faces. As the present exhibition shows, Hockney has been an accomplished portraitist from the 1960s (the ink portraits display his great skill and sensitivity to the sitter). The work he did with the camera lucida enabled him to work with a great variety of individuals, to scrutinise faces of all ages and types. One of the compelling aspects of the portrait show is the great range of individuals - parents, lovers, National Gallery attendants, famous actors, playwrights, authors, designers and artists. It is an organic, unpretentious celebration of life and acceptance of mortality.

Armed with this knowledge of the subtle ways in which every feature varies from person to person, the task of finding a likeness no longer carried with it the anxiety that it might once have had for him. Confident now that he could capture this aspect of any sitter, he was free to turn his attention to other matters both visual - tone, colour, texture - and psychological.

Painting the whole figure rather than just the head and shoulders and then multiplying it by two, and doing so on a nearly life-sized scale, Hockney knew that the resulting portraits would have a commanding presence and complexity. Taking pride in the fact these meticulously observed and naturalistic figures were made without any cameras or photographic references, he had found a fresh and lively way of making portraits by hand for the 21st century.[8]

In *David Hockney: Painting on Paper* (London, 2003), Hockney points out that after the publication of Secret Knowledge, further optical experiments were carried out and a film made for BBC Omnibus. Hockney's conclusion was that 'the hand is now returning to the camera, through the computer. It all leads me back to painting'. The artist acknowledges that two exhibitions were important influences on his new body of work: the exhibition of Chinese painting at the Metropolitan Museum in New York (2002) and 'The American Sublime' (2002) exhibition at Tate Britain, which he attended three times. Hockney has always been attracted to the open spaces of the American West. In the 19th-century paintings on show at the Tate, he identified that there was, in fact, a quality missing. He realised that it was concerned with the fact that the task of the artists and photographers who accompanied the geological expeditions into the new frontier was primarily to 'record'.

In 1860, photography was in its infancy, then being only 20 years old, and was revered as being able to capture 'truth'. Consequently, painters imitated photographers and, in doing so, removed any sign of the brush or the artist's hand. The same occurred in academic painting in France; and yet, from about 1860, artists such as Monet and Cézanne put texture and subjective response back into their painting. A major influence for Impressionist artists was Japanese art, a non-Western view. It is to Chinese art with its bird's eye view that Hockney has recently turned for a more 'human' touch or evocation of landscape. His choice of other subject matter, such as bonsai trees and cherry blossom, and his feel for the decorative elements of a picture, all support another way of seeing than the tradition Western view. 'David Hockney Portraits' is a testament to the intelligence, integrity and humanity of the artist's life and work.

JMcK

References
1. Steiner G. *On Difficulty and Other Essays*. Oxford: Oxford University Press, 1978.
2. Howgate S, Stern Shapiro B, Glazebrook M, White E, Livingstone M. *David Hockney Portraits*. National Portrait Gallery, London, 2006.
3. White E. The Lineaments of Desire. In: *ibid*: 48.
4. *Ibid:* 49.
5. Notes on Sitters. In: Howgate S, Shapiro BS, Glazebrook M, White E, Livingstone M. *Op cit:* 222.
6. He can see deeper than the skin. Interviews by Natalie Hanman. *The Guardian*, 8 September 2006: 15.
7. Hockney D. Foreword. In: *David Hockney: Painting on Paper*. London: Annely Juda Fine Art, 2003.
8. Livingstone M. Sitting for Hockney. In: *ibid*.
9. Livingstone M. David Hockney. In: Morphett R (ed). *Encounters: New Art From Old*. London: National Gallery, 2000: 157.
10. *Ibid:* 158.
12. He can see deeper than the skin. Interviews by Natalie Hanman. *The Guardian*, 8 September 2006: 14.